CAN YOU DO IT STANDING UP?

A DIFFERENT POSITION ON RELATIONSHIPS

Insight To Help You Make Better Relationship Decisions!

KENNY PUGH

Can You Do It Standing Up? A Different Position on Relationships

Copyright 2011 by Kenneth Pugh

ISBN: 978-0-9847017-0-4

Kenny Pugh, LLC

P.O. Box 43064

Atlanta, GA 30336

Visit my website www.kennypugh.com

Cover Design: Tricia Taylor

Interior Design: Chat Kafe

Editor: Nicole Lester

Content Consultant: Donna Berry

Cover Photos: Arthur Butler (Urban Poshture)

Cover Stylists: Carmen Harris (Love Over Logic), Michelle Hoskin (Miche Consulting)

All Scripture quotations, unless noted otherwise, are taken from the Holy Bible, New King James Version.

Printed in the United States of America.

For information send inquiries to:

PO Box 43064, Atlanta, Georgia 30336, E-mail: info@kennypugh.com.

DEDICATION

I dedicate this book to my Lord and Savior Jesus Christ who helped to breathe inspiration into me so this book could become a reality. I am nothing without You and value the purpose for which You created me.

I dedicate this book to my parents Jerry and Betty Pugh who helped model the realities of marriage to my brother Jason and me. Your perseverance has given me a realistic view and expectation of what's to come in the lifelong journey of marriage. When things get tough, I'll be able to reflect back upon the lesson that long-term decisions can't be made due to temporary circumstances. I LOVE YOU!

I dedicate this book to everyone who desires to experience relationships in a way that results in unconditional and uncompromising love. I promise that YOU have the ability to experience the kind of love that can be shared and transferred from generation to generation. I pray for those of you who have not seen healthy models of love, relationships and marriages. This book is intended to provide you with insights to help you make better relationship decisions.

To: Danielle

I hope my book is
a blessing to you.
Continue to work
towards GREATNESS!!
😊

TABLE OF CONTENTS

Introduction

I would like to start by extending a heartfelt thank you for picking up my book *Can You Do It Standing Up?* By doing so, confirms that you are a friend, family member, supporter, you have an interest in learning how to build healthy relationships, or your interest has been piqued by the title. Whatever your reason for picking up this book, I'm extremely excited because you are getting ready to explore a different viewpoint and position on relationships and the positive influence healthy relationships can have in our daily lives.

Unfortunately, relationships in our society have deteriorated to a point where an alarm needs to be sounded to bring attention to the hurt, anger and low self-esteem that is being transferred from generation to generation. I have accepted the role of leading this movement and would like to encourage you to join me on this journey as well.

Allow me to establish some fundamental rules for you to keep in mind before you dive into the first chapter.

1) I am a Christian, so I write utilizing the Bible as my foundation and its principles shape my belief system.

2) Relationships are not only limited to interaction between men and women for intimate exploration. Relationships in this book will include family relationships, friendships, and workplace relationships in addition to those of a romantic nature.

3) My personal experiences may differ from yours. It's okay for us to not agree 100%, but do know that I offer my thoughts from years of interviews, research and counseling sessions with individuals of various backgrounds, marital statuses and socio-economic classes.

It is my goal to challenge the traditional thinking of both men and women to invoke changes in behavior, so we can progress towards healthier relationships for individuals, families, communities and our country.

Upon completion of this book, you will be better prepared to take an unbiased look at yourself, family relationships, friendships and romantic relationships.

I propose the root of life-impacting relationship issues can be addressed if everyone who reads this book begins by analyzing the person they look at in the mirror each morning. Join me as I take you along a path that might make you happy, sad, frustrated or maybe even mad. However, please know that I truly care about making our households, communities and employment environments better places for you to be a part of.

Please join me as I take you on this journey...

Chapter 1

Contemporary Dating Has Destroyed Our Society!

I have gone back and forth debating, arguing and persuading various individuals on my dating perspective with varying degrees of success. Due to the powerful influence of today's society and culture, it is almost impossible to convert the thinking of the 20, 30 and 40-year old individuals about something they personally practice. I once paraded around adamantly declaring my anti-dating stance, but was often met with opposition from others seeking to disprove my perspective. After deliberating the core discussion points I've had with others, the main source(s) of contention centers on terminology and semantics. As a result of my introspective review, I have modified my anti-dating stance and will compromise in an effort to convey my perspective.

I will simply redefine my perspective as *purposeful dating* versus today's *contemporary dating*. Purposeful dating is more aligned with the old school mentality of getting to know someone before heading down the path of courtship (to be defined later). However, *contemporary dating* is practiced by about 97% of today's population. As a result, *contemporary dating* seems to be a significant contributor to today's troubled relationships. There is no coincidence that the lack of truly getting to know someone prior to holy matrimony has led to the inflated number of divorces we see in our society.

A friend and I were discussing the impact of divorce on our society in relation to *contemporary dating*. The first thing I found interesting was the lack of discrimination divorce has on our society. It cannot be traced to race, economic class, religious association or profession. However, you can often trace divorce to two individuals who practiced *contemporary dating*. The following constitutes the definition from which I base all of my research and evaluation.

Contemporary Dating – A casual relationship with no predefined purpose initiated through casual acquaintance and often substantiated by physical attraction. This simply means that you meet someone at the club, grocery store or any other place and feel your interest piqued by his or her physical appearance. However, physical appearances can often lead you astray from a person's character, which is the source of who they really are.

Casual sex, false love, selfish desire, displaced boundaries and miscalculated friendships are all characteristics of *contemporary dating* and serve as catalysts that seek to uproot the foundation of true relationships. *Contemporary dating* has left our society with the following challenges for upcoming generations to overcome:

1) Increase in sexually transmitted diseases (STDs)

2) Increase in the number of children born out of wedlock

3) Increase in single-parent households (meaning parents of children born out of wedlock who never marry)

4) Increase in the number of divorces

5) Decrease in the number of healthy relationships to model after

The first three challenges can be directly correlated to the amount of casual sex that takes place as a result of *contemporary dating*. Society promotes sex as a way for two consenting adults to be personally fulfilled while in a relationship. However, the problem with casual sex is that it places an emotional cloud over relationships, causing a natural detraction from fully nurturing and developing a relationship. It is virtually impossible for two people to remain on the same page relationally when the sex boundary has been crossed due to its emotional influence. Once sexual emotions enter into a relationship, it is difficult to balance the physical attachment (for men) and the emotional attachment (for women). As a result, we've seen ongoing relationship breakups leading to an increase in STD's, unplanned pregnancies and single parenthood.

The last two challenges can be attributed to two people never really getting a chance to learn and know one another prior to making a marital covenant. In today's society, we might as well take "until death do us part" out of the marriage vows. The following may actually work better:
- "until he or she gets on my nerves"
- "until he or she loses his/her job and finances get tight"
- "until he or she doesn't satisfy me sexually"
- "until he or she no longer has the popularity or power they had when we first got married"

I could go on and on, but you get the idea. Healthy relationships are rarely experienced in our society as a potential result of *contemporary dating*. Contemporary dating serves as an uncompromising, self-centered hobby that gives us an opt-out clause once we get upset or bored. We then take the opt-out clause into marriage where many people have chosen to invoke it. We keep practicing the same ritualistic habits, expecting a different result, which is the working definition of insanity.

I know you are probably thinking to yourself "What is the alternative?" Well, let me offer that men and women need to learn how to "do 'it' (relationships) standing up." Continue reading and open yourself up to a new way of thinking that will change your life forever.

Chapter 2

Can You *Do It* Standing Up?

It is absolutely amazing to me how many people strategically utilize sex to attract attention from those they have an interest in. Unlike many of the leaders in our country, I am not ashamed to acknowledge my past active sex life. As a matter of fact, I periodically reflect over my past sexual escapades and recognize it as a very important point of reference for my life. I don't reflect on these moments with pride or with a sense of accomplishment, but rather as an opportunity for further growth and spiritual maturation. I now acknowledge the detriment of pursuing sex in pre-marital relationships. I believe that, in relationships, commitment is very important before surrendering your heart, mind, soul and body to another individual. If we had more commitments, more specifically marital covenants, we would have better families, which would lead to better communities.

That's why I am so passionate about the *Can You 'Do It' Standing Up?* message I share with both men and women. I have had my share of sexual experiences and often chuckle at the various attempts women use to temporarily shift my focus. Why? Because I understand that physical fulfillment comes a dime a dozen. The question I now pose in response to sly sexual advances is **"Can You 'Do It' Standing Up?"** I challenge you to pose the same questions to those who try to enter into your life.

Allow me to make this quick public service announcement to all of the men and women who feel compelled to utilize their bodies as bargaining tools for establishing relationships. **No matter how good you think your sex is there is someone out there who is perceivably better than you!** Now before you become offended, the previous sentence may not have been meant for you so please continue reading...

15

Insight for Women

From the standpoint of pure-sexual experiences, most men will admit that there is no sex better than **NEW** sex. That's why it's dangerous to become involved in relationships where sex is the staple holding it together. Let a beautiful woman with an attractive body cross the path of the 'boyfriend' who doesn't truly care about YOU or value your friendship. The prospect of pursuing, entertaining and ultimately conquering the new challenge is much more exciting than dealing with you as the 'old faithful.' You could be doing **EVERYTHING** right, but will be left heartbroken if he doesn't operate through a source of conviction or if he is unappreciative of the value you bring to the table. That's why it's important for you to ask him the question, **"Can You 'Do It' Standing Up?"** A man who can bring you spiritual covering and fulfillment standing up is worth much more than one who can ONLY lustfully satisfy you lying down.

Insight for Men

Now, I won't let the women off the hook because there are a number of women who are also driven by their lust. Their actions and pursuit of sexual diversity is similar to that of the reality television stars which leads to heartbroken men. I think we often overlook the women cheaters, which is unfortunate because female unfaithfulness does play a part in the downfall of some male-female relationships. If you allow the wrong focus to stimulate a woman's interest, you may find yourself in a situation where your quest for a serious relationship is camouflaged through a buddy status or an informal 'maintenance man' association. Before getting involved with the next woman, be sure to ask, **"Can You 'Do It' Standing Up?"** A woman who brings you peace while standing up is worth much more than one who can ONLY lustfully satisfy you lying down.

Can You 'Do It' Standing Up?

What do I mean by 'doing it' standing up? The reality is there are men and women in almost every walk of life capable of bringing you happiness lying down. Each of us who has had a positive sexual experience can submit personal stories to support this. However, sex alone doesn't make for a successful relationship. How many times must you go through the same test where you figure out the person you are dating is ill-equipped to satisfy you standing up only after having given yourself to him/her physically?

Your focus should now center on following God and connecting with the man/woman who brings you happiness through non-physical means. Stop allowing yourself to remain in emotional bondage to relationships that hinge on 45 minutes – 1-hour (on average) sessions of physical intimacy with a boyfriend/girlfriend. There are 24 hours in a day and 45 minutes to 1-hour pales significantly in comparison to the other 16 hours (24 hours/day – 8 hours of sleep) of involvement with someone who doesn't make you happy. Don't fail the same test again!

Next time ask if he or she can 'do it' standing up? Here are some examples of what I mean:

1) Can he/she demonstrate a love for God?
2) Can he/she demonstrate a commitment in any area of life (e.g. family, work, social group, etc.)?
3) Can he/she show the love of God in their interaction with others? (Matthew 25:35-40)
4) Can he/she offer godly counsel to you as a friend? (Psalm 1:1)
5) Can he/she forgive those from their past? (Matthew 18:21-35)
6) Can he/she show support for the things that are important to you?
7) Can he/she show the ability to resolve conflict?
8) Can he/she produce a vision for the future?
9) Can he/she communicate effectively?

10) Can he/she show continual desire to improve in every area of life (e.g. spiritual, financial, professional, physical, emotional and mental, etc.)?

'Do It' Standing Up Point of Application

'Doing it' standing up has far greater impact on your purpose in life. Two satisfied, emotionally healthy people coming together with purpose are much more powerful than two individuals who are solely looking to fill a physical or emotional void. This means you have to find happiness and purpose in your singleness in order to bring value into a marital relationship. Don't allow a temporary sexual release to blind your ability to make good, sound life decisions. If you keep doing the same thing over and over, you'll continue getting the same results!

Chapter 3

The Communication Gap

Recently I had an opportunity to participate in a relationship discussion that brought together the minds of men and women from various walks of life. The event included those who have never been married, those who were divorced, the young and exuberant and those who seemed to have given up on love. We had a very free flowing dialog that included sex, friendships, biological clocks and communication.

As much fun as it was to discuss the topic of sex, we spent the majority of the discussion focused on communication. One of the women in attendance brought the book *The Five Love Languages*.[1] Although many of the people in attendance had never read the book, most of our discussion emphasized the importance of why a book such as *The Five Love Languages* has significant value.

Communication is a very important piece in bridging the gap between the minds of men and women. Far too often men speak, but women hear something totally different than what is intended. Women speak and men miss out on the subtle emotional nuances of what she is truly saying to him. Why? God has wired men and women in very different ways and our differences cause us to struggle with reaching common understandings. Based on my experiences, women communicate verbally and emotionally and need details to obtain clarity and understanding. On the flipside, men are simple communicators who don't provide much in the form of detail at all. Our responses tend to lack feelings, which lead to barriers when communicating with women. Where does

---

[1] Gary Chapman (2010), "The Five Love Languages: The Secret to Love That Lasts. Northfield Press.

this leave us? It often leaves men frustrated about the amount of information being asked of them by women, and leaves women totally unclear on the message being communicated by men. What's next?

Well, it's important to gain a better understanding of how to bridge the gap in how men and women communicate. Here are a few tips that will help you improve your communication with the opposite sex:

For Women:

Men speak more with their actions than they do with their words. This is a potential catch 22. Men show interest by taking you out, spending time with you, making time for you within the priority of things that are important to him (i.e. business, sports, family). If you want to know if he's interested in you, ask him. However, make sure his actions correspond to his answer. If he says he likes you, but doesn't make time for you, then take it as "He's just not THAT into you!"

Men are not necessarily interested in the details, just the answer. Too much information has the potential of causing men to drift off or shut down. Men don't want to go around the block if the destination is right across the street.

Men have trouble interpreting your emotions or feelings. If you are upset, then say so. If your feelings are hurt, then say so. If you have desires that you want him to address, then lay them out. Otherwise, he may be totally clueless about what you really want him to acknowledge.

Men don't regularly offer-up additional details. If you want to know something specific, then ask the specific question you want answered. If you want to know if a guy is interested in pursuing a relationship with you, don't ask "Do you like me?" Instead ask, "Do you have an interest in pursuing a relationship with me?" Liking you and wanting to pursue a relationship with you are two very different things.

For Men:

Women enjoy details of situations and thoughts. One and two word answers work when dealing with male friends, but it drives women insane. Be mindful to include details that she may be interested in. It may not seem relevant for you to include, but women love being able to create a complete mental picture.

Women don't like short answers when it comes to relationship and friendship status discussions. Be willing to expound upon your thoughts, feelings and desires towards her early in a discussion. Otherwise, you may find yourself in a line of questioning until you answer the specifics of her question(s).

Women enjoy when you share your feelings. Don't be afraid to say, "I miss you," "I was thinking about you," "I really care about you," etc. It may seem a little awkward in the beginning because of how men are naturally wired, but sharing your feelings allows you to speak a language that most women understand.

Women generally have emotional desires connected to their statements. Be intentional in trying to understand the true message she wants you to receive. If she tells you that she had a hard day at work, it doesn't necessarily mean she's looking for a solution. All she may truly want is for you to listen with a compassionate ear.

'Do It' Standing Up Point of Application

Communication is a very important part of any friendship or relationship you are involved in. Remember that men and women are incapable of reading your thoughts, so be willing to plainly outline what you are thinking, what you need from the person who is listening to you and the desired outcome. Doing the aforementioned will drastically improve every relationship in your life.

Chapter 4

Don't Get It Twisted – Lust is Not Just a Man Thing!

One of the questions I've been asked by several women is a very thought provoking one...'Are there any men willing to accept a woman's preference to remain abstinent?' This question is asked because there is already a perceived shortage of quality men in existence. It is valid because if you place another seemingly impossible requirement on your potential mate, will you ever be connected to him? The answer is simple, I've found that there are men inside and outside the church who desire to live a life of purity and who wish to adhere to the commandments of God. There are some men that will require your encouragement and guidance along the journey, but isn't that a key component of what a spouse does?

You have to outline your desires upfront and establish boundaries that are clearly defined to any potential candidates in your life. Men are visual creatures and will typically encounter greater turbulence in the pursuit of purity. The main point is to be able to evaluate a man's *heart* and not become sidetracked if he has a momentary moment of weakness. ALL men (including non-churchgoers, casual churchgoers, ushers, preachers, deacons and other church leaders) will test your boundaries at some point during the journey. Remain committed to your convictions!

Also, ask yourself this question, "Have I gained any advantage by giving myself sexually to the men I was with in the past?" If you are currently unmarried and not a virgin, then the answer is NO! The men you have sexually connected to in the past have taken a piece of you that you can no longer retrieve and you only have experience to show for it. Unfortunately, sex often negatively prolongs the destiny of a relationship headed for failure. There is no correlation between giving yourself sexually and the success of relationships. None! Not only do you connect yourself to someone who is undeserving, but you also disappoint God who watches over you.

Keeping my evaluation balanced, I have also come to find out that many women will test boundaries in this journey, which proves purity is definitely a responsibility shared by both parties. Throughout my journey I've had experiences where I've gotten caught-up in a temporary weak moment and had to be re-focused by the woman I was with. I have also been *tested* by women I have gone out with and had to reject sexual advances that were made towards me. At the end of the day, it takes two dedicated individuals to pursue relational purity. When one is weak the other one needs to be strong and vice versa. We call this ACCOUNTABILITY!

Is anyone perfect? NO! So if you stumble during your pursuit, then get yourself up, brush yourself off, repent and get back on the road that you know God desires for you. IT IS AN ONGOING STRUGGLE AND IS NOT EASY!!! However, God always provides a way of escape for difficult and compromising situations. During potentially intimate moments your cell phone may ring, you may receive a text message from a friend, the Holy Spirit may convict you, but you have to be willing to recognize the signs when they appear. There is a constant war between our physical desires and our spirit. The Apostle Paul describes it best in the Book of Romans.

Romans 7:14-25 (NIV): 14 We know that the law is spiritual; but I am unspiritual, sold as a slave to sin. **15** I do not understand what I do. For what I want to do I do not do, but what I hate I do. **16** And if I do what I do not want to do, I agree that the law is good. **17** As it is, it is no longer I myself who do it, but it is sin living in me. **18** For I know that good itself does not dwell in me, that is, in my sinful nature. For I have the desire to do what is good, but I cannot carry it out. **19** For I do not do the good I want to do, but the evil I do not want to do—

this I keep on doing. **20** Now if I do what I do not want to do, it is no longer I who do it, but it is sin living in me that does it.

21 So I find this law at work: Although I want to do good, evil is right there with me. **22** For in my inner being I delight in God's law; **23** but I see another law at work in me, waging war against the law of my mind and making me a prisoner of the law of sin at work within me. **24** What a wretched man I am! Who will rescue me from this body that is subject to death? **25** Thanks be to God, who delivers me through Jesus Christ our Lord! So then, I myself in my mind am a slave to God's law, but in my sinful nature a slave to the law of sin.

'Do It' Standing Up Point of Application

The Apostle Paul shares with us information about the never-ending battle. Our human nature will try to detour us from doing what we know to be right from a spiritual perspective. However, don't give up and don't give in, you can overcome whatever challenges are placed in your path.

Chapter 5

If It Doesn't Fit, Don't Force It!

Time and time again, God has reminded me that only He has the ability to orchestrate the footsteps of our lives. Unfortunately, in a quest for personal focus on self and the desire to create successes on our own, we make the mistake of trying to force something that He never ordained or intended for us to experience.

I have taken much ridicule about the process I promote for relationship development. However, I continue to hold strong to the view that we were never meant to casually date according to the ways we see demonstrated in our current society. If the current methods were working, then we would see a lot more success stories than we do. The way today's dating model is constructed causes people to inadvertently put the cart before the horse making us better practitioners of divorce, than healthy contributors to relationships. It is impossible to operate in a fully committed relationship without having some knowledge of the person you are connecting to. Thus, confirming the need to operate as friends before exploring any other level of relationship. I know, the dreaded 'friend zone' is one of discomfort and sometimes frustration, but it really does expose the true reality of who someone is. Also, the dreaded friend zone gives you the benefit of assessing whether or not a relationship may truly fit in the lives of two people.

Do you want to learn how someone communicates? Do you want to learn how someone operates under adversity? Do you want to see the habits of a person? Allow them to operate in the friend zone for a period of time.

The friend zone gives two people the opportunity to build a foundation before adding any other complexities into the relationship (e.g., sex, commitment, other superficial expectations). The keys to relational success hinge on the ability for two individuals to communicate effectively, operate under the same values and beliefs, and resolve conflict (see Chapter 3 – Communication Gap). Without these core pieces in place, any relationship you pursue will struggle. Fortunately, establishing a true friendship gives great insight into communication, beliefs, and conflict resolution.

'Do It' Standing Up Point of Application

The message of this chapter is simple...

Most failed relationships can be prevented if two people pay attention to the signs. If it is revealed that a relationship isn't a good fit, then don't try and force it! Otherwise, you'll only have yourself to blame for making an erroneous and anxious decision based on desire rather than destiny.

Chapter 6

The Friend Zone Guide for Women

In the previous chapter I dealt with the 'friend zone' from the perspective of allowing it to serve as an incubator for developing your friendship with the opposite sex. To reiterate my stance, I wholeheartedly agree with the friendship approach to developing healthy relationships.

However, there comes a point where a person has to accept where he or she stands in the life of a person. It's amazing how many women often find themselves caught in the unfortunate extended position known as the friend zone. It is the uncomfortable position that causes you to become temporarily suspended between the platonic origin of friendship and the desired, blissful destination of a romantic relationship. Unfortunately, all women ARE susceptible to this position or state of being. The friend zone does not discriminate based on looks, financial status, spiritual maturity or intelligence.

As a woman, you are guilty of nothing more than allowing the wiring of your innate desire to read into signs that may or may not be true indicators of the interest level a man has for you. What are some of the signs to look for in order to assess whether or not you fall into this category? Consider these:

- You have established a great friendship, have grown to learn so much about his personal life, you find him attractive but things have been this way for months...maybe years!
- You talk to him regularly and the pattern of communication resembles that of two people in a relationship.
- You find yourself reaching out to him when exciting things happen in your life, but his reaction never confirms anything other than platonic or brotherly joy for you.
- You are someone he feels comfortable going to for advice about various

areas of his life, but he never includes you outside of a consultative role.

- You serve as a sounding board for the successes and/or challenges he experiences in his other relationships.
- You have had outings (e.g., lunch, dinner, coffee) with him, but there is never a clearly defined romantic or intimate *feel* to them.
- You are often introduced to others in a way that is difficult to interpret - "This is my girl!" (said in the sister-like tone), "This is someone very close to me", etc.
- You seem to never have a settled feeling on where your relationship stands with him.

The above list highlights some signs that indicate your candidacy for the friend zone. A man may never be forthcoming about his feelings towards you even though he fully understands that you may have an interest in him. Many men are willing to accept what you offer them and may choose the cowardly option of NOT addressing the situation as long as you don't bring it up. Because he has not made a direct signal to you, he feels no obligation to clarify the situation.

Also, if a man never makes a direct move at trying to spend time with you, it is an indicator that he does not have an intimate level of feelings for you. Once he becomes proactive at initiating opportunities to spend time with you, you can then begin processing his intentions for your friendship/relationship.

Don't make the mistake of reading too much into a friendship because more often than not it will result in disappointment. When you absolutely have to have an answer to the question that's burning deep inside of you **JUST ASK HIM**! However, be prepared for the disappointing answer you are likely to receive. No, he's not too shy! No, he's not in denial! No, he's not gay (well maybe not)! The reality is he's just not that into you!

'Do It' Standing Up Point of Application

Fortunately, the story doesn't end there. Once you learn where you stand in the life of a person, accept it and move forward. You want to connect with someone who wants you just as much as you want them. Relationships are beautiful when there is positive reciprocity and I encourage you to appreciate someone who provides this for you.

Chapter 7

The Friend Zone Guide for Men

The previous chapter was entitled The Friend Zone Guide for Women. I'd consider it relational malpractice if I didn't provide a similar guide of direction for men.

We (men) too can often find ourselves in the position designated as the 'friend zone.' As defined in the previous chapter, the friend zone is the uncomfortable position that causes a person to become temporarily suspended between the platonic origin of friendship and the desired, blissful destination of a romantic relationship. The friend zone does not discriminate based on how handsome a man is, the size of his bank account, how spiritual he is or where his multiple degrees were attained. Most men are very uncomfortable in the friend zone and will only willingly accept it in preparation for a future power move or opportunity, similar to a strategy employed in a game of chess. Sometimes we have a very high view of ourselves thinking that we are exempt from rejection. However, as a man and contrary to popular belief, you too can be placed in the friend zone.

As a man, you may find yourself interested in a young lady who has captured your eye with her beauty and your heart with her sensitivity and grace. Unfortunately, no matter your approach (respectful or disrespectful), the woman who you have your eyes set on does not reciprocate the intent in which you approached her. You may be nice, you may be charming, you may be spiritually grounded, BUT for some reason she is just not that into you. Most men accept the unreciprocated response as rejection and move on with their lives. Others may embrace the woman's decision as a temporary setback and begin strategizing the next move in the game known as cat and mouse. How can you tell whether you have been placed in the friend zone? Consider these:

- You have established a great friendship, have grown to learn so much about her emotional desires and drives in life, you find her beautiful, but things have never progressed past the level of *buddy* status!
- You talk to her frequently and the pattern of communication resembles that of two people in a relationship.
- You serve as a sounding board for the successes and/or challenges she experiences in her other relationships.
- You are often introduced to others as her brother or friend, but your non-public interaction seems to resemble something much deeper.
- You find yourself plotting the right time to approach her again, even though deep inside you realize that it's a risky step that has already resulted in disappointment.

The above list highlights some signs that indicate your position in the friend zone. Unlike men, women are generally more forthcoming with their feelings so your standing in her life should never be difficult to figure out. Unless she is in a deeply committed relationship, you may be permitted to remain in her life as a friend.

'Do It' Standing Up Point of Application

Is it possible to break out of the friend zone? The answer is YES. What are the odds of you breaking out of the friend zone? It is very unlikely. There are glimpses of hope during a woman's season of vulnerability, but once the emotional equilibrium is restored, you will likely reclaim your seat in the friend zone.

One thing to keep in mind is to cherish the friends who are in your life. Not all friends are meant to move beyond that purpose in your life. Sometimes we have to recognize that people may be placed in our lives to provide an example of the type of person we should be on the lookout for.

Chapter 8

Are You The One?

One of the most popular debates in the area of singles is the perceived imbalance between the number of available men and women. Before I continue forward let me first put out this disclaimer. NOT EVERYONE WILL HAVE THE OPPORTUNITY TO EXPERIENCE MARRIAGE!!! You have to first resolve within yourself that you are okay in your time of singleness and that you are content with the state God has placed you in. Once you accept whatever God's Will is for your life, you are then eligible for the blessings that He wants to bestow upon you, which may include marriage.

Now that I have gotten that out of the way, let's continue. In the city of Atlanta, for example, the ratio of women to men ranges anywhere from 8:1 to 15:1 depending on the source of information. On the surface the numbers look very lopsided and depressing, but I'd like to offer up another perspective...ARE YOU THE ONE??? It is very daunting for women to agonize over the thought of having to compete with 7 to 14 other women for the shot at a relationship with one man. Over the years I have entertained many discussions about this topic, but would like you to ponder the question, ARE YOU THE ONE? As a male entrenched in the process of identifying and sorting through the many options that are available for men, I have noticed that 'quantity' of women has NO correlation to the 'quality' of available women. In evaluating the lopsided ratio of women to men, I can say without a shadow of a doubt that a large number of women are unqualified candidates for healthy long-term relationships. I know ladies, men have issues too and I will deal with that in upcoming chapters. Men's issues can often be isolated to fear of commitment or lack of desire to excel in life. For the sake of conversation let's say the ratio of women to men is ~10 to 1.

Let's look at the categories that most of those 10 women fall into:

1) **Low Self-esteem** – Men can sense when a woman is a member of the low self-esteem club. Wholeheartedly, quality men are NOT drawn to women with self-esteem issues because they are often considered liabilities in the relational big picture. Insecure and abusive men ARE drawn to women with self-esteem issues because they are in search of someone they can control.

   Quality men like to know that they are connected with a woman who is able to stand firm on her own and not demand/require constant affirmation. Now don't get me wrong, a good man will speak words of encouragement to his woman and does not mind speaking life into her aspirations and goals. However, men would also like to know that they are in a partnership and not feel like they have a father-daughter dynamic in their relationship. Women with low self esteem can be spotted typically as someone not having a strong male figure in their lives growing up (this is not absolute), someone who has been taken advantage of by loved ones or someone whose family structure never allowed them to feel valued. Women with self-esteem challenges should first get rooted in God's Word so they are able to understand who they are in the eyes of God before seeking connection with a man.

2) **Bag Lady** – Unfortunately, men are not always accepting of women who bring children into the equation of relationships. Several of my closest friends have decided that they do not want to have to deal with the inherited 'baby's daddy' in developing a long-term relationship with a woman. They want to be able to share the experience of having a child together for the first time and not feel as if its 'old hat' for the person they are with. On the flip side, there are many men (myself included) who do not have a problem developing a relationship with a woman who has children.

   The second bag lady group is comprised of women who seem as if they transition from one relationship to the next without disconnecting or purging themselves of 'hazardous waste' (including trust issues, preconceived notions and old memories) detrimental to future relationships. As the internal time clock begins to tick in the lives of some women, we sometimes notice a haphazard transition from one relationship to another in search of Mr. Right. The danger of doing so leads to many negative articles of luggage being transferred from one relationship to the next with no possibility of success. Bag ladies need to embrace their season of singleness and allow God to purge the unhealthy thoughts, experiences and expectations from their lives.

3) **Ms. Too Independent** – You know Ms. Too Independent. She is college educated, volunteers in the community, earns a good living and is a faithful servant in the church. All of these things make up the beautiful resume shell that most men would kill for, right??? Hold on! The aforementioned qualities ARE awesome and most men desire these in a mate. However, let's insert the qualities that do not show up on the resume of that quality woman submitted for review by a potential mate:

   a. She may be the one with the inability to compromise on issues,
   b. She may be the one who lacks the helpmeet skills to make a man feel valued
   c. She may be the one who cannot cook or clean and demands to eat out all of the time
   d. She may be the one who cannot leave the authoritative drive it takes to be successful in Corporate America out of the household.

   Just because you are an attorney, doctor, IT manager or marketing director does not mean you can carry the authoritative demands into the household. These are the negative qualities of women that usually drive good men away. Unfortunately, Ms. Too Independent makes up the bulk of seemingly qualified candidates who have it going on according to the expectations set forth by society. However, these women are considered exceptions when discussed in the intimate circles of men. Ephesians 5:22 (NIV) "Wives, submit yourselves to your own husbands as you do to the Lord" is a good verse to meditate on in preparation for a God-ordained relationship.

4) **The One** – This is the woman who carries the same characteristics that

Ms. Too Independent possesses, but she is not overly flamboyant or loud about her personal resume or successes. She operates powerfully, but with a silent aura of confidence that gives no other choice but for a man to respect her. She is willing to go to bat for her man and shows desire to make a harmonious partner in the household. She exudes the characteristics of the perfect woman, and understands that progression towards becoming the woman God has called her to be is a continual process. She is able to get her man to open up; she offers a shoulder for him to cry on and does not act as if she 'knows it all'. Men typically retract themselves into a shell if they feel their relationship partner lacks the listening skills that men so desperately cry out for in relationships.

'Do It' Standing Up Point of Application

Don't concern yourself with ratios because that will surely depress you. Fortunately, God does not work in the form of ratios or according to earthly odds. Continue developing yourself, building and allowing God to shape you so that you are the one!!!

Chapter 9

Worth the Wait

In 2007, as I stood in line awaiting the opportunity to cast my vote for the next President of the United States, I began reflecting on something that resonated within me spiritually. At the beginning of that week I began assessing the various voting locations and associated wait times in order to decide when and where I would cast my ballot. In the area where I live, the various early voting locations had waiting times ranging from 2 to 6 hours. Because of the importance of the election, I decided to pick a location, jumped in line and waited for 2 hours and 47 minutes until I was able to accomplish my goal. I forfeited my desire for a shortcut and persevered through the twisting and turning of a line containing hundreds of individuals. I was eventually able to accomplish my goal and it was indeed worth the wait.

When you reflect over your life, most things you have achieved came with a process. Many of you had to endure 16 years of education in order to achieve your college degree. Many of you had to endure 18 years of life prior to transitioning out of your parent's house in order to live on your own. Many of the successful marriages you hear about required years of experience in order to achieve a level of harmony and happiness.

What am I trying to say? Many of you are willing to endure some level of process in life in order to achieve goals that are important to you. However, in other areas of life you seek a shortcut to your desired goal. If relationships and marriage are important to you, why would you want to usurp the process in order to engage in one outside of God's will? If education were important to you, why would you seek a shortcut to avoid the process of learning? If growing spiritually is important to you, how can you justify not reading your Bible and spending time with God daily?

'Do It' Standing Up Point of Application

Don't allow your impatience to convince you to do something that IS NOT in your best interest long-term. Focus solely on God and your priorities, and you will endure the process needed to attain the goals you desire.

Chapter 10

Relationship Intangibles

It's hard to believe, but even after you have acquired a Bachelors, Masters or PhD, there is still no guarantee that your relationships will be successful. Many of us have been misled into thinking that a college degree, money in the bank, corporate career and prestigious awards are the foundation of successful relationships. Over time, I've witnessed the rise and fall of many relationships based on tangible things. With the success many women are now experiencing academically and in their careers, there is a sense of expectancy that many of them carry into personal relationships. Newsflash! The intangibles (a.k.a. the little things) are what make for successful long-term relationships. Intangibles can include, but are not limited to: 1) being a caring person, 2) being a gentle person, 3) being a selfless person, 4) bringing peace into relationships, 5) being a patient person, 6) being a loving person etc. How many of you evaluate your potential life mates based on the aforementioned intangible characteristics? Men with money and women with beauty are easy to find because they come in abundance. Will they be there for you when you are down and out? Will they remain with you after being laid-off from a job? Will they console you when you experience sadness in your life? Will they remain patient with you as you go through your personal growing pains? These are the questions you need to be able to answer when evaluating a potential mate.

My friend put it best a long time ago when he recommended that I only accept applications from 'B-students' when searching for my wife. You may be asking yourself what is a B-Student? Glad you asked. A B-student is the one who never received an abundance of attention while in school, but always did quality work on every assignment. They are the ones who didn't receive the top academic awards, but were always successful in everything they did. What does this mean to you? For men, 'A-students' are the beautiful women who receive an abundance of attention everywhere they go. A number of them are defined by their beauty and have no self-esteem outside of their beauty. Why do men say the pretty girls bring the most drama along with them? Men say this because pretty girls are sustained by external accolades and not internal sustained sufficiency. For women, A-students are the overachieving men who are sustained by accomplishments and public acknowledgement. They lack the sensitive character makeup needed to be successful fathers and good husbands. A-students are able to provide for you financially and can buy you some pretty awesome gifts, but in the end lack the ability to love and care for you as you deserve.

'Do It' Standing Up Point of Application

The real question that you need to ask yourself in all relationships is "Would I be happy growing old with this person without money, possessions or public acknowledgments?"

Your answer to this question should give you some direction on how to proceed forward with the person you're evaluating. The person you decide to partner your life with should be someone that brings happiness without all of the material items, influence of power or accolades. Imagine being stranded on a deserted island with him or her and assess whether your friendship could bring you a lifetime of love, joy and happiness!

Chapter 11

The Best Valentine's Day Date Ever!

Let me tell you about the best Valentine's Day date I ever experienced. Allow me to set the stage for you.

The weekend was absolutely awesome! I had confirmed a date with someone I know very well. This person also knows everything about me. This person has been with me through the ups and downs of my life. This person knows how to finish the statements I creatively contemplate in my mind. This person has seen the good and bad of my relationships and worked through the healing process of hurt.

I had the perfect outing planned for us too. We attended church service at 6:00PM. It was immediately followed by a nice dinner outing at an urban bistro. After sharing thoughts over a nice entrée, the night concluded with a time of wonderful relaxation and exchange of personal thoughts. It was great spending time with someone who is 100% behind your personal goals and aspirations.

Would you care to know whom my date was with? My Valentine's Day Date was with ME, MYSELF and I!

'Do It' Standing Up Point of Application

If you cannot learn to enjoy and appreciate yourself, then you will never be prepared for the ONE God wants to send into your life. Don't let commercialized holidays define who you are, be willing to enjoy life no matter what season you are in. Life is short...so enjoy it!

Chapter 12

False Start Relationships

Many people are being disqualified from the relationship race towards marriage because they are running in races God never cleared them to start. In the sport of track and field, the race officially begins when the starter gives the starting orders (on your mark...get set...) and concludes with the firing of a gun (GO!). At the sound of the gun all participants in the race are cleared to run and give their best because they've been cleared to start. If a runner happens to start before the sound of the gun, the gun sounds again resulting in a false start warning and places him/her on the road to disqualification. In some races, the runner is automatically disqualified even after one false start.

'Do It' Standing Up Point of Application
Many adults in our society are in the starting block of relationships, anticipating the firing of the starting gun. However, instead of listening for the starting sound from God, they find themselves hearing alternative starting signals (i.e. lust, looks, wealth, power, sex). They mistake these for an official clearance from God. God typically provides people the opportunity to retake their position in the starting blocks, but few ever do. As a result, the disqualification for having successful relationships is evident in our society as confirmed by our divorce rates, single parent households and the lack of value placed on the family structure. Let's wake up people!!! We have time to get it right, but let's break the chain of bad decisions and living for physical satisfaction.

Chapter 13

Relationship Formula for Success

It is an undeniable truth that many of you desire to pursue relationships and experience the God-ordained covenant of marriage. In order to do so, there is a formula that embodies the totality of what relationships should be made up of.

God + Your Significant Other + You = The Success of Your Relationship

God
Fortunately, God is the same yesterday, today and forever more. As a result, you cannot and will not go wrong by putting your trust in Him. God serves as the anchor in your relationships if you allow Him to do so. As long as He remains your primary focus, you will be able to endure the highs and lows, ups and downs, good times and bad times of dealing with other human beings. Men and women have the ability to change; God does not! Without God, you will find yourself relying on your flesh to maneuver and operate through the everyday trials of relationships.

Your Significant Other
You have the opportunity to screen, interview and ultimately hire the person you allow into your life. Don't be in a hurry, don't ignore the red flags and don't allow your emotions to assist in making life-changing decisions that you may regret later. Seek God's guidance, take your time and enjoy the process of learning about your potential mate through the course of everyday life. Rushing to the altar is probably not the best answer! Allow your relationship to endure the various seasons of life so you have a better picture of what you are getting into long-term. Ask God to give you the spiritual discernment needed to make a wise decision.

You

Ultimately, you are the only person that you can control in all of your relationships. Take time to assess what you bring to the table in all of your relationships (workplace, family and male/female). You should set periodic assessment checkpoints to evaluate where you are in the following areas of life such as:

1) **Spiritually** – Where is your current relationship with God? Are you spending time with Him daily? Are you growing spiritually?

2) **Emotionally** – Have you purged the hurts of past experiences and relationships?

3) **Physically** – Are you taking care of yourself physically? When is the last time you had a physical? Do you exercise regularly?

4) **Financially** – Do you have your finances in order? Do you have a budget? Do you have a plan for eliminating your debt? Having a solid financial life doesn't mean you need to make a lot of money. It means that you have control over the money you make.

5) **Mentally** – Are you continuing to develop yourself educationally? What was the last workshop, seminar or class you took to improve YOU?

'Do It' Standing Up Point of Application

Use the current season of your life to make yourself the best person you can be. Don't wait for Mr. or Mrs. Right to come into your life before you assess your personal areas for improvement. God is in the process of molding the person He would like to send you, but wants you to be prepared for whom He sends. Life is short. Live it up and be the best you can be!

Chapter 14

Reality of Love

The reality of love is this: We don't have the ability to really love without the power of the God working through us.

In 1 John 4:7-8, we are taught "Beloved, let us love one another, for love is of God; and everyone who loves is born of God and knows God. He who does not love does not know God, for God is love." According to this scripture, we don't have the capacity to love without God giving us that ability as we surrender ourselves to Him.

So how are people able to love when they don't know God? Well unfortunately they can't. At least they are not able to love with the type of love God demonstrates. God's love is a special kind of love that the Bible calls "agape". It is a love that flows out of the will of God and does not change. It does not change based on feeling, emotion or attitude. It is the most stable and predictable kind of love and the only type that can provide a lasting foundation in marriage and other relationships.

Often, when people say they love someone, they are just talking about sexual desire or a passionate feeling. These kinds of feelings fluctuate regularly and are not synonymous with pure love. Modern day love outside of God isn't strong enough to endure the many storms of life that relationships and marriages experience.

Agape love, however, is a committed and sacrificial love that is modeled after Jesus. When Jesus tells us He loves us, He isn't talking about a feeling that comes and goes. He is telling us He is committed to us forever and will not change. He loves us regardless of whether we are a drugaholic, alcoholic, sexaholic, lustaholic, workaholic or any other -holic you can name. Jesus' love for us remains the same no matter what we do to Him. We really need to consider what we mean when we tell our spouse, fiancé/fiancée, boyfriend/girlfriend "I love you". Are we saying that we are experiencing an emotional feeling when we are around them or are we saying we are committed to him or her forever and will demonstrate love regardless of bad feelings or negative circumstances?

People controlled by their emotions are unreliable and their instability can do a lot of damage to relationships. Relationships built on personalities and moods are destined for failure. The most stable and dependable people in relationships are those who are submitted to the influence of the Holy Spirit. They are powered by a supernatural love that will lead them to do the right thing through thick and thin.

'Do It' Standing Up Point of Application
Your desires can be fulfilled. Ask God to fill you with the power of His Holy Spirit. He never intends for us to go around trying to love people out of the shallow well of our own emotions. The ocean of His love is always available to any of us who would just admit our weaknesses and depend upon Him. His agape love is the highest love and will transform any person, relationship, or marriage under its influence.

Chapter 15

Breached Relationship Boundaries

One night I had the opportunity to speak with a friend about an uncomfortable situation she experienced regarding an ex-boyfriend. She and her ex-boyfriend had not communicated regularly since their breakup several years ago, but he reached out to her due to a death her family recently experienced. Even though the initial call was to serve as a source of encouragement, he used this as an opportunity to re-connect with someone he had history with. To complicate matters he contacted my friend again to share an intimate dream he had about her. Now this may not seem too out of the ordinary, but this ex-boyfriend is now married with a family. The nature and timing of his call was shocking and caused discomfort within the spirit of my friend. Fortunately, she did the right thing by not entertaining the conversation and not feeding into the potential trap that could have presented itself.

As I sat and listened to this scenario, I began to ponder the various men and women who remain in contact with individuals from their pasts. The above scenario highlights a married man approaching an ex-girlfriend. However, some married women are just as guilty of remaining too close with ex-boyfriends. Here are some questions I began to pose:

1) Is there anything wrong with remaining friends with ex-boyfriends or girlfriends?

2) Upon entering into a serious relationship, do you discuss past relationships with him or her and request boundaries to be implemented?

3) Are there dangers of remaining connected to an individual you have a history with?

4) If you are friends with an ex-boyfriend or girlfriend, how do you keep the contact appropriate?

'Do It' Standing Up Point of Application

Remaining too close with someone you have history with serves as a potential source of discord and contention with the new person you're trying to develop a relationship with, which can lead to breached boundaries.

There is nothing wrong with maintaining friendships with ex-boyfriends or ex-girlfriends provided proper boundaries are established. One of the first things to consider is whether the previous relationship has the potential to pose an issue in your current or future relationships? The questions listed above are ones to consider ensuring you maintain proper boundaries before moving forward into new relationships.

Chapter 16

Married and Miserable vs. Single and Sexless

I have come to the realization that our generation has some serious flaws and gaps as it relates to marriage and dating relationships. I look all around and notice that the number of failed relationships and marriages seem to dwarf the number of positive relationships and marriages. Why is that? Is it because men decide that marriage doesn't seem worth the headache after having already committed? Is it because the number of men and women coming from stable two-parent households has pretty much become non-existent? Is it because men, like me, wait so long to consider marriage that selfish habits and ways settle in as roadblocks against our desire for marital bliss? Is it because many of the women we seem to attract give us the full experience of marriage-like privileges without the need for a ring or commitment?

As a man, the options for evaluating the God-sent ONE seem to be numerous in quantity, but scarce in quality. The options appear in many shapes and sizes; they are Christian and non-Christian, they represent various professions and educational backgrounds and possess many skills and gifts. However, there is no amount of money, no level of beauty or no gift outside of God's love that can replace being blessed with THE ONE God has chosen for you.

A friend asked me to name the number of married couples between the ages of 25 and 40 years of age whose marriages I would model mine after. I couldn't really answer the question with optimism, but came up with a very short list of individuals. Unfortunately, in the requested age group I can name way more couples that are married and miserable.

Maybe I am focusing too myopically! My sad reality is that married and miserable has become the unfortunate face of what bachelors like me have in our presence to contaminate our thinking. If marriage is so good, then why are so many people trying to get out? Why do so many married people seem married and miserable? Has the enemy's selfishness crept in to disrupt what God has created as good? Do men and women stick around simply because they have become numb to their unhappiness? Why are single women the only ones who seem gung ho about marriage? Is it because they've never tasted it before and once they do, the excitement will dissipate?

The other alternative is to remain single and sexless. The Bible speaks against premarital sex and preaches abstinence with consequences for your disobedience. Awwww dang! That's not the alternative I want to pursue long-term either! Let me reflect and be realistic. I've had enough sex during my teenage, college and early adult years to last a lifetime so will I really miss it? Lord, all I can say is please deliver me from me.

I don't want to become consumed by this season of life because each year of singleness adds to the already constructed wall of self-consumption in my life. Single and sexless. Well this does allow me time to focus on life without the cloud of emotional entanglement associated with unauthorized sexual relationships. After all, God deserves so much more and at the end of the day; it's not about me, but ultimately about giving Him the glory! I haven't received confirmation on being called to a lifetime of singleness from God so I will continue developing myself, continue pursuing relationships and following Him for my direction on marriage.

I seek to discover the purpose that God has for my life and pray and trust that He has included the marriage chapter that I desire so much. I hope God allows me to surround myself with positive married role models that can help mentor me as I seek to explore that area of my life. I thank God for providing my parents and grandparents as role models for marriage. Despite what goes on around me I can always look home for the structure that is outlined in the Bible.

'Do It' Standing Up Point of Application

No matter if you remain single or transition into a marriage relationship, it is imperative to position yourself to be the best you that you can be. Think positive thoughts and make the most of your status no matter what it is.

Chapter 17

Are You Prepared to Receive?

Many people today ponder the question, "When will I meet the person I will spend the rest of my life with?" The better question for people to consider is, "Am I really prepared to receive the person I will spend the rest of my life with?"

Here are a few areas of your life that should be ongoing works in process in preparation for your life mate.

1) Spiritual – Do you read God's Word and fellowship with Him regularly? Why would God send you a mate when you haven't established a regular relationship with Him? Are you asking God to send you a mate when you can't even commit to Him? (James 1:7-9, Psalm 107:1-2)

2) Physical – Do you take care of yourself? Do you get enough sleep to remain healthy? Do you eat healthy and regularly? Do you exercise regularly to stay in shape? When is the last time you have had a medical checkup and dental exam? (1 Corinthians 6:19-20)

3) Professional – Do you have a plan to continue growing professionally? Or are you comfortable with simply having a job? (2 Timothy 2:15)

4) Financial – Do you know what your credit score is? Do you operate from a financial budget? How deep is your debt and would someone feel comfortable connecting to you and your current debt situation? (Proverbs 3:9-10, Matthew 6:33)

5) Social – Are you a homebody and not open to social things? Do you fellowship with friends? Do you participate in church, professional and/or friend gatherings? (Deuteronomy 6:4-6, Acts 2:46-47, Proverbs 27:17)

6) Mental – Do you read regularly or is your growth based on television?

Do you have any hobbies or outlets for your stress? (1 Timothy 4:13-16, Colossians 3:23)

'Do It' Standing Up Point of Application

Becoming the right person is just as important as connecting with the right person. One thing my mentor taught me is that too many singles don't understand how important the areas listed above are. If you can be effective in the listed areas, it puts you in a great position to be successful in marriage. If you struggle in any of the areas, be sure to make specific areas of weakness and your needs known to God. Allow Him to continue working and maturing you in those areas while preparing you to become the best you can be for your future mate. Two broken vessels coming together do not equal a whole relationship. However, two whole vessels coming together will result in one strong relationship.

Life is too short for you to become complacent in your thinking and being. Continue moving forward in life because there is so much God wants you to experience. Do not allow life to be taken for granted!

Chapter 18

Do Professional Black Women Face Dating Hurdles?

Dating for professional black women is one of the most interesting debates that we entertain in today's social circles. In my opinion, I believe we have made the issue a lot larger than what it truly is because of the many books, movies and workplace discussions that deal with the subject. When truly evaluating the core issues at hand, the hurdles that professional black women have fishing in a relatively small dating pond are as follows:

1) **Media Influence** – The media has truly influenced the perspectives and self-views of many professional black women. When a message is conveyed over and over again, it often positions the recipients to begin embellishing the statements as truth. You hear messages regarding the issues professional black women face in dating via radio shows, blogs and magazines. This prompts the discussions between friends, co-workers and thus results in the perpetual mindsets that now exist. The reality is no matter if the statistics state that 42.7% of African-American women are unmarried, women have to realize that it only takes meeting ONE man to place them in the 57.3% category. However, if a negative mindset is embraced, then negative experiences usually follow.

2) **Misconception of Men's Views** – There is a misconception that men are intimidated by the educational, professional and social statuses of successful black women. This is true when women are only exposed to groups of insecure and immature men who lack motivation. If this seems to be the norm, then I recommend doing something different in order to get exposure to new circles of men. There are groups of men who desire to be men of integrity. There are men who desire to be married. There are men who embrace the professional and educational pursuits of black women. There are men who desire to love women unconditionally. The common misunderstanding of black men is that "black men are intimidated by successful black women." The success isn't what disconnects men and women as implied by this statement, it's the perceived attitude that is associated with the professional

success and education. If two people make each other feel valued, then the relationship will work despite an educational or professional gap. Genuine love bridges the widest of gaps and eases the deepest of insecurities.

3) **Misunderstanding of "Value"** – Somewhere along the line of time our society lost the things that should be viewed and embraced as "valuable" in relationships. Say what you want, our grandparents were able to build long-lasting relationships not based on money, but on love and sacrifice. By having one another's back through thick in thin. By understanding that sacrifice will get you further than a master's degree, home or diversified financial portfolio. When you need someone to hug, to vent to or sacrifice during your time of need, a person's net worth is irrelevant. Don't get me wrong, it is important to have goals and pursue them, but not at the expense of losing a grip on what keeps relationships anchored.

'Do It' Standing Up Point of Application

Professional black women may encounter greater distractions in some cities than others, but this can be attributed to the social competition and materialism that exists. Smaller cities don't typically have the same level of competition and thus a different relationship mindset exists.

Professional black women do face hurdles when dating, but much of it lies in the distance between their ears. A renewed mindset, confidence and an understanding of what is truly valued in relationships can make all the difference in dating and relationship experiences.

Chapter 19

When the Chase is Over

Periodically, I am reminded of the many relationship mistakes I have made over the years. I try to downplay and claim convenient amnesia regarding the number of mistakes that have transpired in my life, but God keeps them fresh in my mind in order to maintain changes in my behavior. One of the things men as a whole enjoy is the chase or pursuit of a woman they want to learn more about. All through high school, college and even into my early professional life I aligned myself with this practice, but failed to address another very important element in relationships. What happens when the chase is over?

Once the chase or pursuit comes to a halt, another major crossroad is reached and one has to assess whether to be satisfied with the woman he has worked hard (or somewhat hard) to connect with? Or do you declare victory and press on towards the next challenge? Far too long I opted for the latter because of the chess match and adrenaline rush that accompanies each new pursuit. As many men have stated before, "There is no feeling like claiming victory with a new woman." Unfortunately, the result of this theory positioned me to always be on the lookout for the next challenge, curiosity or relationship pursuit. Is this representative of a fear of commitment? Some may say yes...but I adamantly say NO! I call it a bad case of the male curiosity syndrome.

Curiosity is one of those things that work as an asset in life because it leads to the discovery of new things. It can also serve as a liability because it can place you in a position of split-second decision-making and progressive trouble. My mother used to tell my brother and me "Curiosity kills the cat!" Her warning simply meant that more often than not, our curiosities in life will lead to trouble.

'Do It' Standing Up Point of Application

Fortunately, my curiosities have not yet killed me, but have positioned me to take a hard look at seriously evaluating when the chase is no longer worth it. To all men, I also encourage you to take the challenge of evaluating the importance of the chase and when it becomes detrimental to your overall purpose in life. There is a call going out for more men to abort the pursuit of the chase and accept the call to commitment and greater character. Are you willing to accept the call? I am!

Chapter 20

You Need a Commitment!

How many of you know someone in a relationship that seems to be going nowhere? How many years must go by before making a commitment or deciding that other options are desired? Today is the day where you decide that some type of commitment is required from your 'friend' or significant other. It is no longer good enough for you to wait while he or she finds himself or herself. It is no longer good enough for you to wait while he or she figures out what he or she wants to be when he or she grows up. It is no longer good enough for you to wait while entangled in a relationship with someone who hasn't figured out whether or not they want you. It is time for you to have a grown-up conversation that will either solidify the direction you are both going in, or frees you up from a relationship that will **WASTE VALUABLE TIME IN YOUR LIFE.**

Life is an asset that has a predefined expiration date. You cannot add to or take away from the allotted time God has prescribed for you. Understanding this, why would you remain ensnared in a relationship that doesn't align with your future aspirations or desires? It is time to make a firm decision to only allow those with like minds and goals to remain connected to you. If your 'friend' or significant other is not progressing towards the big picture goals you have for your life, then it's time for you to set them free. Life is too short to remain connected to people who will hold you back from what God has purposed and birthed inside of you. Take control of your life and continue towards the destiny God has called you to. Be blessed!

"Every day that you waste delays you from progressing towards your destiny!"
--Kenny Pugh

'Do It' Standing Up Point of Application

Don't settle when you have the ability to soar. I guarantee you can fly higher when connected to someone who encourages and empowers you to be ALL you can be. Conversely, you'll never reach your goals if you remain grounded by dead weight that will only hold you back. Uncommitted relationships are a form of dead weight that can keep you from being all God has designed you to be!

Chapter 21

Compatibility Questions

Although there is no 100% guaranteed way of predicting if a relationship will be successful, there are some key factors to consider when interviewing a potential mate.

Please consider these as good starter questions to ponder and evaluate if your relationship has the potential for success:

- Do we share the same religious beliefs?

- Do we share similar family experiences, upbringing and desires (kids vs. no kids)?

- How does my potential mate view and manage finances?

You will never have a firm foundation in your relationship if religion, family views and money management are out of alignment. Differing views on any of the above questions are cause to truly reconsider pursuing a relationship with your counterpart. If the aforementioned questions bring about differing viewpoints, it may be good to seek counseling if you believe the relationship is serious.

Here are some additional compatibility questions that one should consider when evaluating a potential life mate. Please don't minimize the importance of these questions as they could lead to conflict down the road in your relationship.

- Will one or both of you work when you start having kids?

- Who will retain primary responsibility for managing the checkbook and household finances?

- Does your potential mate allow his/her **family** to become too involved in your relationship? If so, are you willing to deal with this for a lifetime?

- Does your potential mate allow his/her **friends** to become too involved in your relationship? If so, are you willing to deal with this for a lifetime?

In continuing with my look at compatibility questions to consider when evaluating a mate, please consider these:

- How does your new love handle a crisis? – There is nothing worse than finding out that your life mate becomes abusive, dependent on drugs or alcohol, or experiences extreme depression when crisis occurs. You may not have an opportunity to personally experience crisis with your mate during the dating/courting/engagement phases of your relationship. However, be sure to engage in intimate dialog that may be able to shed light on how they have dealt with crises in the past.

- How does your new love behave in public places? – Does your potential life mate become extremely obnoxious towards you or others in public? Does he/she treat common workers (waiters, waitresses, doormen, custodians, etc.) rudely? When a person demonstrates a lack of respect towards people, it could be a warning that this lack of respect may one day include you.

- How does your new love treat your friends and family? – Have you ever seen a situation where a spouse did not get along with a parent or friend of their husband/wife? It makes for a very uncomfortable situation and could be a source of friction throughout the duration of the relationship. Be careful and try to resolve conflicts quickly so they don't linger.

I pray that the compatibility questions shared above will help prevent potential roadblocks in your relationship!

'Do It' Standing Up Point of Application

Remember, do not seek ways to kill a potential relationship, but look for ways to confirm you have the right person. Make sure you ask all of the key questions necessary to learning all you can learn about the person you are considering sharing your life with. Marriage isn't easy, if it was everyone would be doing it a lot better.

Don't look for characteristics in a person that you are not willing to exhibit yourself. There is only one Jesus...so please manage your expectations for your mate. No one is perfect, but make sure they are intentional and willing to follow the perfect Christ.

Chapter 22

Uninvited Guests

The more I research the topic of relationships, the more confirmation I obtain about the number of complexities men and women bring to the table in pursuit of healthy relationships. Most recently I explored the following question: "How can seemingly good men or women still be single?" Well, upon further review I've realized that men and women can appear to be good externally, have their material and professional ducks in a row, but a number of their relationships are eventually derailed by uninvited guests.

Now you may be sitting there with a perplexed look on your face, but many of us (myself included) have at some time brought some uninvited guests into our relationships. It's a good time to see if you can personally relate to any of these. If not, then share with a friend, family member or co-worker.

For Men

Memories of Desperate Women – One of the quickest ways for you to disqualify yourself from being blessed with a Proverbs 31-esque woman is to bring memories of past desperate women along with you. Unfortunately, too many men feel as if ALL women are desperate and will do just about anything to say they are in relationships. This may be true for women with low self-esteem, who are uneducated or who lack proper guidance. However, women who bring education, self-esteem, self-sufficiency and a desire for relational partnership to the table are more interested in building a future than catering to your past. What does this mean for you? It means that you must be willing to embrace the progressive, entrepreneurial and successful mindsets in exchange for the insignificant, irrelevant female ego-boosters from your past.

For Women

'Outside' Male Advisors – One of the quickest ways for you to escalate the anger level in a man is to emasculate him by placing too much focus and faith in outside male advisors. I'm not saying that you shouldn't solicit information from men you value in order to guide you through situations. However, I am saying that you should allow men to grow, mature and develop through experiences without constantly comparing them to your fathers and/or pastors. One of the most frustrating situations from a man's perspective is to have another man with significant input in your relationship when it's unsolicited. I say this especially to women who hold their pastors and ministers in high esteem. Please remember that your man/fiancé/husband is the one who needs to be empowered to make decisions in your household. Your pastors and fathers each had the opportunity to learn through individual experiences, so please don't remove this opportunity from the men in your lives. I know this may not sit well with some of you and that's okay. I'm simply sharing the message for you to contemplate.

'Do It' Standing Up Point of Application

As challenging as relationships between men and women are, we cannot afford to keep bringing uninvited guests into them. Take time to examine your past relationships to see if there were any situations where uninvited guests were allowed to creep in? If so, be mindful of allowing this to happen in the future. Even though we all have influences that we respect in life, please don't allow them to hinder the growth of the person you are involved with. If you allow the natural process of relationships to take place, it can make for a much more valuable and appreciated experience. Leave the uninvited guests at home!

Chapter 23

Unequally Yoked - Are You Connected to the Wrong People?

I can say with absolute assurance that most everyone who reads these words has been connected to people who once upon a time were detrimental to your growth and development. To be unequally yoked means to be connected or tied to someone who does not have the same beliefs, desires and/or goals as you. Many misinterpret this idea as only being relevant to marriage relationships. However, this idea of being unequally yoked applies to marriage relationships, business partnership, as well as purposeful dating relationships. Why is it important to avoid being unequally yoked to others in your life?

1) **Unequally yoked relationships can provide what is known in the medical field as a false negative.** False negative tests give the appearance that whatever is being tested for seems to not exist in the person being tested. It gives the sense that things seem to be okay when in reality they aren't. How does this apply to being unequally yoked? Well, unequally yoked relationships give the appearance that things are okay in your life because everything on the surface seems fine. However, if you look under the surface, the association is actually harmful for you. To further clarify, this means you find comfort in associations that seem good externally, but are destructive to you internally. You cannot continue to keep people in your life who make you feel good, but don't add any value to your life.

2) **Unequally yoked relationships also promote added fatigue in your life.** Do you feel tired continuously? It could be because you are trying to carry too many people in your life. Healthy relationships consist of two people who are willing to offer equal support, encouragement and empowerment to one another. If one person is doing all of the work in the relationship, then it promotes an added level of fatigue in the life of that person. In various types of relationships there is a natural fluctuation in who is giving more than the other because of our

humanity and the impact of external situations in our lives. However, healthy relationships navigate through this fluctuation and provide an acceptable flow of give and take between people who appreciate one another. Please remember that we are designed to operate with sails and not be bound by anchors that keep us from soaring in life. No wonder people are experiencing fatigue; they are worn out from carrying too many people around in their lives. Does this describe you?

3) **Unequally yoked relationships prohibit you from reaching your potential.** There is something to be said about a person's associations in comparison to the level of success he or she experiences in their endeavors. There is a popular saying that goes a little something like this…"Birds of a feather flock together." This means people of like minds, purposes, beliefs and successes often associate with one another. However, highly successful people often seek out opportunities to connect with people who are more successful so knowledge can be obtained. Are you the most successful person in your circle? If so, then you need to identify some more people to associate with. Wouldn't it be a tragedy for you to never reach your potential because of the company you keep?

'Do It' Standing Up Point of Application

When you allow yourself to be unequally yoked to those who don't add value in your life, you receive false negatives, you experience fatigue and you could fall short of reaching your potential. Why allow yourself to go through this when you have the ability to change and control your associations? Resolve within yourself to take inventory of your current associations and determine whether or not you need to make some changes. It's important to reach the God-given purpose you've been created to achieve. Be willing to make the necessary changes so you can be all you can be. Be equally yoked in all areas of your life!

Chapter 24

All Hope is Lost for Women Over 30

I'm glad I'm not a woman who has progressed past the seemingly taboo age of 30 without the slightest hint of a suitable marriage partner. Seemingly, all hope is lost for women who fall into the category of over 30 seeking a husband! Why? Women have been taught since an early age that life's pinnacle is reached once you complete your education, establish your career and experience marriage, which is the foundation to starting a family. What many of the people feeding into the minds and spirits of young girls at an early age neglected to tell you was the first two goals could be accomplished independently; whereas, the last goal involves participation and cooperation from another responsible and willing human vessel.

It is very easy to buckle-down and focus as an individual on overachieving academically and professionally because many of the challenges you encounter can be overcome through personal motivation and perseverance. However, the process of joining with a husband or wife is a bit more challenging and requires divine intervention. Interestingly enough, the inability to obtain marriage 'on-demand' is something that is now frustrating the minds of women and driving down the self-esteem of many women across the country. This dilemma is being experienced not only in major cities like Atlanta, Chicago, Miami, New York and Los Angeles, but also in smaller cities across America.

Many women have achieved success from an academic and professional standpoint, but yearn deeply to find the missing puzzle piece that may have been passed by during the process of pursuing greatness. Whose fault is it? You have done all that was asked in order to position yourself as a 'good thing' to be found as referenced in Proverbs 18:22 "He who finds a wife finds what is good and receives favor from the LORD." Whose fault is it? Being ashamed of achieving academic excellence in a time when men are unable to keep pace is displeasing. Whose fault is it? Having goals and dreams should not penalize you from experiencing the full-life you were taught to pursue. Is it your fault? Absolutely not!

How does a woman rebound from a twisted perspective introduced by today's society and remain focused on the things in life that truly matter? Can I help you with this?

'Do It' Standing Up Point of Application

Your breakthrough doesn't lie in the form of the popular television shows, magazines or advice from your girlfriends. Your breakthrough will come after you decide to relinquish control of the very things that are not in your power (Matthew 6:33). You may be able to control your personal pursuit of academic excellence. You may be able to control positioning yourself for career opportunities through diligence and dedication. You may be able to control the process of superficially filling the void of marriage through your selfish pursuits. However, you cannot control the love-filled, God-honored, God-ordained union of marriage as described in Scripture because it is a GIFT that is arranged, orchestrated and confirmed by God. However, all hope is not lost in your pursuit! You just have to shift your focus, take your hands off of the steering wheel and relinquish control back to the One who can change your life situations.

Chapter 25

Would You Date You?

We all have desires and characteristics that we would each like our mates to possess. It is very easy to sit back and analyze who comes into your life, checking off the various items that align with your checklist. Unfortunately, many of us do not go through the same exercise of evaluating ourselves in the same manner we scrutinize and assess others. An open-minded person is willing to contemplate the following question "Would I Date Myself?" Better yet, what is your relationship value?

How would you rate yourself in the following areas on a scale of 1-5? Next, rate the areas in order of importance for the person you would seriously consider as the husband/wife in your life.

Meaning...what's important for your mate to bring to the table?

1) **Physical Health** – What is your current physical status? Do you eat healthy? Physical attraction isn't necessarily based on looks, but it is based on your ability to present yourself in a manner that accents you as an individual (i.e., via your attire, grooming, nails, etc.).

2) **Professional Pursuits** – Are you where you desire to be professionally? If not, are you taking steps to achieve your goals? Or are you simply treading water working a JOB? Your professional life is something that you should pursue and stabilize during your single season.

3) **Financial Management** – How are your financial management skills? Do you know how to balance a checkbook? How is your credit? Sound financial management isn't based on how much you make, but your ability to properly manage what you do make. Finances are a major component to the health of marriages, so you need to be able to positively contribute in this area.

4) **Social Skills** – Do you know how to have fun? Do people enjoy being around you? Or are you always negative? Can you enjoy the subtleties of life? Your social life helps bring enjoyment to healthy relationships.

5) **Spiritual Walk** – Do you have a spiritual life? How important is it to you? Are you willing to compromise your beliefs for Mr./Mrs. Right? Your spiritual life is either seen as a major foundation or simply nice to have in relationships.

Check your scores:

25 – Try again…no one is perfect

21-24 – You are a great catch

16-20 – You are a good catch

11-15 – Needs improvement

6-10 – Destined for singleness

1-5 – Is a response really needed?

'Do It' Standing Up Point of Application

You may be wondering why you keep seeing this list of focus areas throughout this book. What I've learned over the years is that all of the areas listed can be worked on during your single season. I can also tell you that ALL of these areas are important for success in marriage.

Chapter 26

Enter Relationships at Your Own Risk

Jesus is the supreme example of living without fear of being disappointed by others: "He emptied Himself by assuming the form of a slave.... He humbled Himself by becoming obedient to the point of death - even to death on a cross" (Philippians 2:7-8).

Disappointed and hurt people sometimes find it difficult to move into new relationships. This is a direct result of being hurt by someone who was able to break through the brick wall often erected by someone who has had a negative past experience(s). Should disappointment and hurt detour us from pursuing future relationships and opening ourselves up to people in the future? Of course not! Remember, all people in their humanity have the ability to disappoint and hurt others because no one is perfect. We should never operate with a spirit of fear towards relationships because that is contrary to what God wants for our lives. Let's face it, all people, even Christians, can be rude, uncouth, obnoxious, and sometimes downright disgusting. After experiencing heartbreak we as unmarried adults may even be tempted to display signs on the doors of our hearts that say, "Enter into a relationship with me at your own risk."

Forgive my sarcasm, but I am not naïve enough to believe Christians and non-Christians are incapable of hurting others! What are we supposed to do when we know that a move toward another relationship exposes us to the risk of being disappointed? We move forward in love, which is easy to say, but definitely difficult to do. Making disappointment a thing of the past and ourselves vulnerable to hurt is frightening, but it has to happen if we are to love as we are loved.

'Do It' Standing Up Point of Application

Mature Christians are those who are willing to look fully into the face of hurt and disappointment and feel it, knowing that because they do, they will come to a deeper awareness that no one can comfort the heart like Jesus Christ. In the presence of such pain, one more easily sees the uselessness of every attempt to find solace in one's own independent strategies. Facing and feeling the pain of disappointment underlines more than anything else, the gripping truth that only in God can we trust.

Chapter 27

Stop Test Driving!

The modern, cultural idea of dating relationships seemingly encourages you to test drive the idea of marriage by modeling the marital structure as much as possible until you get married, or decide it's not a good fit. The latter simulates a pre-marital exploration without a lifelong commitment, and often leads to an emotional divorce with someone to whom you have never been married.

The biblical idea of marriage holds that sexual intimacy should be reserved until after you are married. God encourages this model because true marriage is based on a covenantal view and not a contractual license. Participating in sexual intimacy prior to marriage gives access to your body when it should be reserved for your husband or wife. Biblically speaking, you are looked upon as being married to everyone you've had sexual intercourse with. If that's the case, how many husbands or wives do you have? Ouch!

Also in relationships, you should refrain from establishing too deep of an emotional connection with someone in the early stages of a relationship. It's not that you're being dishonest or cold, it's simply being cautious about living out a deeper commitment than truly exists between you both. Song of Songs 2:7 tells us not to awaken love before it pleases: Do not start what you cannot finish without the presence of sin. Falling in love usually leads to you 'lusting' out of it. However, growing and maturing into love allows you to establish a foundation capable of withstanding the circumstances of life. Stop test-driving the idea of marriage until you are positioned to truly experience it!

Your goal should be to determine whether the person you're dating is the one to marry without having to go through both an emotional and physical divorce if the answer is no. Stop test-driving marriage until you have discerned that God has prepared, positioned and promoted you into it.

'Do It' Standing Up Point of Application

Will there still be disappointment and emotional pain if a "biblical" dating relationship doesn't work out? YES! Any relationship that doesn't lead you to your desired goal has the potential for disappointment. Even the ones that are biblically based will still have levels of disappointment. However, the pain will be lessened by the honest, mutual, spiritual concern for one another that results when two people treat one another like brothers and sisters in Christ first, and potential spouses second. This is for the protection of everyone involved and ultimately glorifies God!

Chapter 28

Dating Dilemma – Part 1

Many people who are close to me understand that I have a unique perspective when it comes to the practice of dating. After conducting an in depth analysis of the Bible, I concluded that 'contemporary dating' is unbiblical. Any attempts we use to connect the Bible to dating are based on assumption and not scripturally supported. Does this mean we shouldn't date? Nope, I won't go to that extreme, but I will offer-up the notion that our perspectives need to change as it relates to the practice of dating. We must make better educated dating decisions and not become lured into the guidelines of contemporary dating set forth by reality television shows.

We have been trained by our society to believe that intimately dating multiple people at the same time is acceptable and the norm. However, when you think about dating, and the end result that we should be working towards, we ought to take the process of selecting a potential mate more seriously. It's difficult enough as it is to clearly engage and assess your compatibility with one individual, but it's exponentially more difficult when you start including additional individuals to assess while being intimate with them all at the same time. In order to date multiple people at the same time, one must truly be grounded in who you are AND have the ability to separate your dating partners without blurring the dating experiences. The truth be told, many of us have barely fully embraced who we are as individuals, which makes dating multiple partners a recipe for disaster. How can you assess your compatibility with someone else when you are not fully stabilized in your own personal being? I've provided a recommendation to many of my close male and female friends and I'd like to do the same for you. Please accept the following challenge in an attempt to better position your dating experience:

1) **Make a decision to only truly 'explore' one person at a time.** This will afford you the opportunity to learn about the person more in depth, and provides them with your undivided attention. You will be able to quickly make a decision on how much time to give them and allows you to break off unhealthy candidates a lot earlier in the process.

2) **Be willing to step out of your comfort zone.** This will give you the opportunity to experience people other than your traditional 'type'. Let's face it; your type will probably get you the same results that you have already experienced in life. Give someone different an opportunity to display themselves to you.

3) **Dating isn't a license for sex.** Refrain from allowing your intimate side to get involved in dating. Sex and physical intimacy clouds your judgment and causes many people to remain in dating relationships longer than they should. Sex sidetracks and distracts your ability to think clearly when evaluating a life mate.

4) **Learn how to date yourself first.** If you don't know how to date yourself, then you'll struggle in your dating relationships. Be confident in who you are and learn the things that make you happy and a quality candidate for a relationship. Don't allow dating to define who you are because you'll find yourself in an endless loop of disappointment.

'Do It' Standing Up Point of Application

The priorities of successful relationships are as follows:

- Your relationship with God
- Your relationship with yourself
- Your relationship with others

If you learn to embrace the order of the priority of the listed relationships, then you'll be positioned for happier, healthier relationships.

Chapter 29

Dating Dilemma – Part 2 (the church edition)

As I continue looking at the dating dilemma, I would like to take a look at dating through the eyes of those who are regular churchgoers. Unfortunately, men in the church are the scapegoats when it comes to the dating dilemma, but I'd like to offer-up my support for the men. Men in the church face some very unique challenges when it comes to dating.

1) **The Ratio of Women to Men** – Unfortunately, the one aspect that is embellished by men all over America can also serve as a detriment. It's sort of like a kid in a candy or toy store, too many options can impede the ability to make a decision (I won't chase this rabbit, but it's tempting). Too many options make it difficult for men to observe and truly collect the data important for making solid relationship decisions. What is the typical result of a man having too many options? He is usually a man who has trouble making a decision and/or making a commitment. Until a man recognizes that there will always be more beautiful, sexy, intelligent women out there, he will continue waiting for the 'perfect' woman, who DOES NOT exist.

2) **Identifying the Best Approach** – Many men get this wrong and it usually shatters their confidence for future opportunities.

   Here is a list of the <u>wrong</u> times to approach a woman for dating inquiries:
   - **Before service begins on the way into the doors of the church.** There is nothing worse for a woman than being interrupted on her way into the house of the Lord in order to receive a Word from God.
   - **During the middle of service by way of a note written on the back of the church program.** What are you here for? This isn't your high school history class, so please pay attention to the preacher and the message. If a woman thinks you are attractive, you ruin it when you pull this foolishness.
   - **At the altar when the pastor or minister is praying for the**

congregation. Please don't try this! I've seen it attempted and it provides an awkward experience for everyone who witnesses it.

Here are some more opportune times to approach a woman in order to express your interest:

- **After church service is over and people are socializing in the hallways, parking lot or sanctuary.** This is a great way to obtain informal information about a person you may be interested in. Take advantage of the informal opportunities for fellowship with your church brothers and sisters.

- **During a church fellowship where the environment is a little more relaxed and the traditional social barriers are removed.** Church fellowships are a healthy alternative to the club life and prove to be more fulfilling long-term. Healthy church fellowships can remove the tainted taste of smoke filled clubs, strip clubs and gatherings that typically lead to a path of unrighteousness.

- **While serving in ministry.** There is no better way to learn about a potential interest, than by serving with her in ministry. I cannot speak directly for Christ, but I imagine He would smile down on His children serving together in ministry while also developing a long-term relationship.

3) **Making a Good Choice** – Many men have experienced this hard fact. In the church body, a lot of women run in similar circles. As a result, if a man has his eye on more than one woman in a circle of friends, he runs the risk of blackballing himself if he selects the one who he isn't compatible with. The only way to avoid finding yourself in this predicament is to sit back and observe the behavior of the women you have an interest in. Based on a more thorough observation you can better assess the woman you may have more in common with, etc.

'Do It' Standing Up Point of Application

Overall, dating is a very challenging process and one most men get wrong. Hopefully, the tips above provide some insight on how to better position yourself for successful opportunities. In the end, God is sovereign, and He will position you to meet the one He has in store for you in His timing.

Chapter 30

Great Mate Expectations!

How long will it take you to finally decide that the many expectations you have for your desired mate are unrealistic? I often ponder this question from a male perspective and it is something that many of us, both male/female, never seem to take a look at until it's too late. If you take a poll of expectations for men and women coming out of colleges and universities, many of them will provide a long list of requirements that need to be met by their mate. However, when you look closely at the many expressed qualities and requirements, it is very difficult for any one person to meet the excessively long list of requirements.

Unfortunately, many men and women hold onto this long list of expectations far too long and carry this list into their 30's, 40's and 50's while their years of singleness increase. How often should we revisit our list of requirements for potential mates? I would recommend at least once or twice of year. You assess (or at least you should) everything else in your life regularly; your desires for your mate should also be included in this ongoing assessment process.

'Do It' Standing Up Point of Application

I have noticed many people, both men and women, settling for mates later in life because they have operated for too long with unrealistic expectations. There is more evidence of this in the church, where men and women add spiritual maturity to an already long list of requirements. There is only one man who has lived a life of perfection on earth (Jesus Christ), so you will not find a mate who can present a resume of perfection. However, it should be your desire to find someone who can help you fulfill the purpose God has for your life. Love, joy, peace, longsuffering, kindness, goodness, faithfulness, gentleness, self-control (Galatians 5:22-23) are great measuring tools for assessing whether someone is a great candidate for a relationship. If he or she demonstrates these characteristics when dealing with you, it speaks volumes about their character. Stop focusing on the material things that you can 'see' in life and focus on the great things a mate can 'be' in your life!

Chapter 31

Let's Wait A While

In 1986, Janet Jackson came out with a popular hit titled "Let's Wait a While" that took the country by storm. The words of the hit song used to epitomize the approach that 'quality' women took when dealing with men in dating and relationships. Unfortunately, things have shifted from "Let's Wait a While" to a "have-to-have it now" attitude.

The modern day approach is pretty predictable and standard. Man meets woman. They exchange information. They go out. Man taps into the mind of the woman or vice versa. The ability to seize control of a person's mind usually results in an open heart and open body experience. It's usually that easy. Unfortunately, when you cross certain boundaries in relationships, it usually leads to a change in appreciation of the relationship. Tupac stated it best in his song "I Get Around" when he said; "I don't want it if it's that easy!" This can be better translated, as "I won't want YOU if it's that easy!"

Now there is nothing wrong with the above formula as long as it's with the person you are married to. However, the above equation has gone from a Hollywood fairytale experience, to a merry-go-round experience with the flavor of the week. Would you share your retirement account with someone who isn't vested? Well, why share ALL of yourself with someone who hasn't made a commitment to marriage? Hmmm...

This leaves me with questions about what roles we play in relationships in today's society.

Have women taken on a more male-minded mentality when it comes to sex? Do women have a 'probation' period before they release themselves physically to someone they're dating? Why NOT make men wait for the prize if you believe it's worth it?

Why don't men take a "Let's Wait a While" approach when dealing with women? Do men not respect women who make a commitment to saving their treasure for marriage? Why don't men value their bodies and who they connect with?

'Do It' Standing Up Point of Application

I wish I had the silver bullet answers to all of the aforementioned questions. However, I posed them in order to prompt personal reflection by you. It's up to you to determine where you fall in relation to each question. It's my hope and prayer that you begin to take on a different position on relationships so you don't continue to perpetuate the same cycles we are going through today.

Chapter 32

Should Women Pursue Men?

How appropriate is it for women to approach men in pursuit of relationships? The 21st Century has brought about many changes to the traditional way things have been done in our society. The evolutions of education, family focus and equality have been influenced by the feminist movement. A sense of independence in women has blossomed as a result of our progressive society causing an ever increasing comfort to pursue whatever their hearts desire. Should this independence include pursuit of men for relationships? Or has this approach proven to be a detriment in the formation of long-term relationships?

My personal position is that it is out of order for women to pursue men for relationships. In most instances relationships begin out of spiritual alignment when a woman becomes the aggressor and removes the innate nature of how God created a man. A man does not typically appreciate a woman he does not have to work for as much as a woman who provides a challenge for him. This is not an absolute truth and I can provide examples of successful relationships where women were the aggressors. However, I can provide many more examples of women who were used and exploited because of their zeal in aggressively pursuing men for relationships. Guys are able to smell 'thirsty perfume' on a woman and will take advantage of this if it is not carefully addressed. Aggression can be misconstrued as desperation and that is where relationship problems begin.

Here are my top 2 reasons why women should not pursue men for relationships:

1) **It Is Unbiblical** – I hate using this reason because it is a religious trump card. However, nowhere in scripture do we see God promoting women as the lead in pursuing relationships...or anything else from a leadership perspective. I know this is a tough pill to swallow, but I am only serving

as the messenger.

2) **Relationship Roles Become Twisted** – God created men as hunters and that is typically the role men are supposed to serve in. We typically don't operate well when we are placed in passive roles and allow women to take the lead. I believe this is why relationships internally combust years down the road in situations where women served as the lead. Guys sit on their true feelings until they reach a point where they literally explode due to long-term frustration.

I've argued in the past why some women pursue men for relationships. Here is the top reason that supports that position:

Men Have Become Passive – As the trend of society has shifted and women are becoming more successful professionally and educationally, men have reverted into passive beings. Unfortunately, the number of 'good' proactive/aggressive men has become limited. As a result, there may be situations where a woman may find it necessary to take the lead in initiating the relationship, but her ultimate goal should be to transfer leadership back to the man in order to avoid conflict further along down the road.

'Do It' Standing Up Point of Application

As I close, I don't want you to take on a position of opposition regarding the pursuit of men. I truly believe that however God connects a woman with a man, His desire for your life must be obeyed. I'd like to have you also consider this example: Men are like hunters when it comes to how they are wired. Most hunters don't take pride in capturing their prey, which is lying on the side of the road. However, men take extreme pride in having to work, stake out, monitor, capture and kill whatever it is they are hunting. This can be applied to pursuit of relationships. Allow the man to pursue and capture you so he feels as if he's worked to earn your association. It's healthy for long-term relationships!

Chapter 33

'Catch 22'

I have recently been reminded why so many guys have trouble sharing information openly with members of the opposite sex. Although communication is very key to friendships and relationships overall, the difference between how men and women are able to understand and reach conclusions is so very different.

I sometimes see why men opt to keep certain things to themselves in that they fade away in the sunset. Unfortunately, things usually float to the surface when it comes to male/female interaction. Contrary to my natural selfishness, I've been sticking to the approach of confronting not-so-fun conversations in an attempt to keep boundaries established and individual/joint purposes clear.

It's funny though. It's a 'catch 22' to share specific thoughts throughout the course of a 'get to know you' friendship because they lead to optimistic thoughts and anticipations that may or may not ever be realized. However, it's also a 'catch 22' to NOT share thoughts with the other person during the 'get to know you' friendship because it leads to a sense of ambiguity and uncertainty.

What's a man to do in these situations?

- Look beyond the temporary discomfort and focus on the big picture.
- Don't allow a woman's emotions to persuade you to keep things internalized. This means it's not good to keep your thoughts and feelings to yourself.
- Recognize that God has a plan beyond our control and we DO NOT have authority to control situations.
- Remember honesty is the best practice in all situations.

'Do It' Standing Up Point of Application

At the end of the day, men need to continue being honest despite the potential for further questioning, elaboration and whatever else is required for situational closure. It's absolutely essential that everyone remains on the same page and no one's time is carelessly wasted. We owe it to women and ourselves to 'man up' and not be afraid to deal with tough situations. Doing so builds character and respect from those whose paths we cross.

Chapter 34

Relationships - Greenhouses and Cheerleaders

Recently, I posted a message on my Facebook page that stated women should be like cheerleaders and men should be like greenhouses. Let me explain this statement further.

I recently had an opportunity to hear a message by a minister who was discussing marriage and healthy roles for each spouse to play. The role illustrations given for successful marriages were those of a greenhouse and cheerleader. Initially this statement caused some confusion, but let's explore in detail. The following is based on my interpretation on what was shared during this session.

A greenhouse is a structure that provides a controlled atmosphere, gives shelter against outside elements and transmits a proper amount of sun and nutrients conducive for growth and bearing of fruit. Likewise, a man or husband should always provide a controlled atmosphere for a relationship because he has the ability to calm down situations that cause anxiety, and inject optimism into situations that seem challenging.

Reflecting on my childhood, I always remember my father being the thermostat in our household. My mother, brother and I could be in the best of moods. However, if my father was upset when he got home from work, all of our moods were altered because of his lead. Conversely, my father also had the ability to bring happiness into an environment that seemed depressing or sad. A man should also serve as protection for his wife and family against outside influences and opposition. No matter what others are saying or what is taking place at

87

school, a wife and children should always feel like the husband/father will protect or take up for them. Correction for inappropriate behavior or improper decisions may take place in the background, but no one outside of the immediate family should be able to attack (physically or verbally) a member of a man's family without a fight (not literally). Finally, a man must provide proper nutrients and sunlight conducive to bearing fruit. This speaks specifically to a man's ability to sow seeds into his family. If a man desires his family to grow and prosper, then he should sow continuous seeds of 1) Fear of God, 2) love, 3) integrity, 4) discipline and 5) wisdom.

As the helpmeet of a man, a woman in a successful marriage is called to be like a cheerleader. In a society where the pressure to protect and provide traditionally falls on the shoulders of men, a helpmeet should always be willing to cheer her man on to victory. All the independent women may interject at this point to offer a counterpoint of interest about their ability to provide for the family too. I do not object to this point because many of today's women are able to contribute to the household needs. However, most men do not marry solely because a woman is able to contribute financially. Most men marry because they find a woman who they believe supports them wholeheartedly and encourages them to accomplish great things. A woman's role is characterized as being a cheerleader because cheerleaders cheer no matter what is taking place during a sporting event.

It's amazing that when my Ohio State Buckeyes were losing in a football game, you could still see the cheerleaders cheering even though the losing outcome had already been decided. Cheerleaders are charged to provide motivation when times get tough and the team feels like quitting. Cheerleaders celebrate when successes and victories occur, but also provide encouragement when things seem a little bleak. Likewise, women should do the same in the lives their men. Men are programmed to accomplish things and pursue goals and victories. Men need a source of encouragement when life doesn't seem to be working out for them.

'Do It' Standing Up Point of Application

Unfortunately, modern-day relationships have transitioned from being a support network to being a battle for position and attention. The truth is that a woman's financial contributions are not enough to offset internal relationship discord. However, a woman's support and encouragement are enough to help persevere through times when relationships endure challenges. The last place a man wants to encounter opposition is at home. Likewise, the last thing a woman wants is a man who doesn't protect and provide for her needs.

Men, work toward becoming awesome greenhouses and ladies, work toward becoming the best cheerleaders you can be. It's an awesome result when the two roles come together as one!

Chapter 35

Sexually Test Drive Your Mate??

1 Corinthians 6:18 - Flee sexual immorality. Every sin that a man does is outside the body, but he who commits sexual immorality sins against his own body.

One of the more popular questions I receive when I state my position on pre-marital sex is "What happens if my mate and I aren't sexually compatible?"

The question is thought-provoking, but there is no clear out-clause for those seeking permission to continue in worldly behavior. Some say a test drive is necessary in order to avoid future infidelity issues between a husband and wife. Some say sex is a major component in a relationship that should not be ignored and left to post-marriage chance. Some say it isn't possible for two people with an attraction towards one another to resist physical interaction. There are several compelling reasons to support the pre-marital sex point of view. However, the one opposing argument I would like to present is 'Do you trust God?' Proverbs 3:5-6 says, "Trust in the Lord with all of your heart and lean not on your own understanding; In all your ways acknowledge Him, and He shall direct your paths." If you trust God and say that you follow Him wholeheartedly, then you have to trust His ability to supply all of your needs...inclusive of your sexual desires.

Sexual compatibility is often viewed as a natural chemistry, which is true. However, sexual compatibility is also something that can be learned and developed through love, faithfulness, willingness to teach AND learn, and willingness to explore new ideas and techniques. The trouble many couples experience is the temptation to compare their spouse to previous partners. You reach a relational pinnacle and now want the husband/wife in your life to live up to the compilation of the many previous sex partners you entertained during your life. How realistic or fair is that? It's not very realistic or fair at all.

'Do It' Standing Up Point of Application

I've also heard it put this way…when you recognize the true value of something, there is no need to test drive or try it out. Bentleys and diamonds are exquisite, but rarely do you see people testing them out for compatibility. However, other types of vehicles and items allow anyone to test them out. What is the point I'm trying to make? Are YOU a Bentley or another type of average vehicle? Do you trust that God has sent you a Bentley or do you think the man/woman in your life to be a Kia? God values when we obey His Word to save ourselves until marriage.

Remember, love is the characteristic many casual sex relationships lack. Love has the ability to take an average, casual sex relationship to an outstanding covenant sex relationship within marriage. Trust God and allow Him to do "exceedingly, abundantly above all you can ask or think…" (Ephesians 3:20). HE CAN DO IT!

Chapter 36

Younger Women vs. Older Women?

One of the dating dilemmas I continue to go back and forth with in my life deals with fully understanding what I TRULY want in my personal relationship. I have dated a variety of women in my life and they have varied in age from 7 years younger to 10 years older than me. It's always interesting because there is a distinct difference in experiences between the two age groups. I often ponder the thought of do I want a younger or older woman? This is an interesting debate and guys often discuss the many benefits and downfalls of each. After all is said and done it basically comes down to personal preference.

In my experience, younger women often offer a different level of energy and excitement that is unique for relationships. There is typically a level of life exploration and innocent pursuit associated with those who fall in this category. On the flipside, I have also experienced an enhanced level of insecurity by women who fall into this category. Unfortunately, a sense of peace, patience, focus and trust are rare, but valuable traits if and when you find them in younger women.

Older women on the other hand are traditionally more settled in their lives and have already experienced some of the things younger women still pursue (i.e., night life, position in society, etc.). Older women tend to be more seasoned with their security and don't engage in discussions often initiated by personal paranoia (e.g. Why aren't you answering your phone? Where have you been? Who was that woman you were talking to? etc.). Older women are usually positioned to move very quickly in pursuit of what they want, which can be both good and bad. Men who deal with women who fall into this category need to know what they want because time for procrastination and playing games is non-existent. Some younger women allow men to string them along in relationships, even when it's obvious they won't ever progress. This is sometimes the case because there isn't the same level of urgency placed on moving relationships forward. On the flip side, some older women have the potential to almost force men into premature decisions due to the race against their 'biological clocks'. It's unfair to make sweeping generalizations, but there are certain trends that can be seen through the experiences of various people (i.e., family, friends, co-workers, etc.).

At my age, if I opt to pursue an older woman, I'll be prepared to move quickly in maturing the relationship, determining our marriage potential and be ready to initiate a family shortly thereafter if we both desire to have children. If I pursue a younger woman, I'll have to be ready to deal with some of the growing pains associated with women who are still in search for their personal direction in life.

'Do It' Standing Up Point of Application

The moral of the story is this...no matter who you deal with they will never be perfect. You have to assess each person for who they are and make a decision on whether they help you reach a level of purpose you cannot reach on your own and vice versa. Relationships are not solely about you, but a healthy compromise between two people looking to build a better future together. Don't look for perfection in your mate, but look for someone who you can always strive to love perfectly.

Chapter 37

Dating and Privacy

When dating you should expect to learn basic information about the person you are spending your time with. Information such as age, occupation, children, likes and dislikes should not be viewed as out of the ordinary. However, there are some areas of life that begin to push the limit of comfort for those going through the 'getting to know you' process (e.g., income, credit score inquiries, number of past sex partners, etc.).

Men tend to be a lot more private/secretive when it comes to sharing information. I think this has a lot to do with a woman's natural desire to learn certain things. Whereas, a man doesn't really focus on things outside of the basics.

1) How private should you be when you are dating someone new and you want to explore a relationship with him/her?

2) At what point during the relationship do you begin to share the more intimate details about yourself with the person you are dating? Are you an open book? Or does someone have to pry information out of you?

3) How do you inquire about a person's family history?

4) When do you address someone's past relationship experiences?

'Do It' Standing Up Point of Application

Each of the above questions are interesting ones to address when growing through the process of relationship development. At some point during the process of getting to know one another you need to begin addressing questions that actually have substance. Our society doesn't need another marriage initiated solely because two people are attracted to each other. It is imperative that you actually know something substantive about someone you desire to spend the rest of your life with. Marriage is not a simple calling to undertake, if it was, everyone would be doing it successfully.

Chapter 38

God's Good Girls

I am writing this to the many women who are trying to do things 'right' according to God's Word. I know I am NOT a woman and I definitely enjoy my masculinity, but I do recognize your current frustration in today's environment of male-female relationships. Just so we are clear as to what my definition of doing 'right' is, allow me to further explain. Here are the characteristics of how God's good girl should operate based on MY interpretation of God's Word.

1) **God's Good Girl** has accepted Jesus Christ as Lord and Savior of her life. (1 John 5:12-13)

2) **God's Good Girl** serves faithfully in ministry and enjoys doing God's work. (1 Cor. 7:32)

3) **God's Good Girl** is actively working to improve herself in ALL areas of life in preparation for the mate God has for her (i.e. spiritually, financially, socially, professionally, mentally and emotionally). (Proverbs 31)

4) **God's Good Girl** has forgiven all of her ex-boyfriends for their relationship failures and has purged all hurts. This includes acknowledging your contribution to the demise of the relationship. (Matthew 18:21-22)

5) **God's Good Girl** recognizes that her body is a temple and protects (doesn't give it away sexually), adorns (dresses respectfully) and preserves it (exercises). (1 Cor. 6:18-20)

Many of my Christian sisters are dedicated and consistently operate according to the principles outlined above. I also want to emphasize that nowhere did I mention that you have to be perfect, so don't place too much pressure on yourself to do so. As we see in Romans 3:23, "All have sinned and fall short of the glory of God." This includes a number of pastors, preachers, evangelists and prophets who act as if they have the ability to walk on water. Don't beat yourself up based on the appearance of how it seems others are living. You continue to focus on your maturation, commitment and God's purpose for your life.

If you fall in the God's Good Girl category and consistently find yourself frustrated because you still encounter relationship challenges, I say do not let your faith waiver. I say to remain focused on the 'main thing' (salvation and Christian living) and allow God to orchestrate the rest. Believe me I know this is easier said than done. Especially, as you watch those around you who operate in a less than godly manner continue to get married. Is there something wrong with you? Should you simply give up on the lifestyle you've chosen to live and go back to 'dating as usual'? It depends...

There are a lot of people who are married, but not necessarily happily married. Don't allow your temporary season of loneliness cause you to make a decision that will make your life miserable. We often get caught-up in the celebration of two people coming together, but rarely share in their misery of a bad mate choice until the relationship is virtually over. You'd rather continue persevering with expectancy in the God who is able to meet your desires, than to give up and rely on yourself to make a flesh-led decision that may lead to further misery. What about the guys who don't want to live with your decision to be abstinent? The reality is many guys won't necessarily embrace the idea (I know this isn't the traditional minister answer). However, you have to make the decision whether you are open to giving someone access to something they don't have a covenant to claim ownership. A LOT OF WOMEN AND MEN DO!

The problem is the attachment and bond that is formed through the sexual act and the inability to see clearly after the act is completed. I DO NOT recommend you eliminate a man just because he makes an advance towards you. There is a difference between making an advance and putting pressure on you. One is a result of being caught up in the moment; whereas, the other is an intentional attempt at making you do something where indecisiveness is present. Whichever the case, I DO recommend that you better manage your boundaries so you don't find yourselves in situations where you have to deal with those advances.

If you've made the decision to follow God and His directives expecting things to operate in your timing, then you're setting yourself up for failure. Everyone I've known that has tried to walk in alignment with God's principles have all reached a point along the journey where they became a little frustrated and began to petition God for direction. However, they remained fully engaged in ministry and God placed someone in their path that they ultimately grew to love.

'Do It' Standing Up Point of Application

I know the journey can be somewhat lonely and another "Keep the faith," "Keep hope alive," and "God has someone perfect for you" proclamation from a preacher may not do the trick. Just remember…there are some God's Good Guys out there who are going through a similar journey as you in their quest for relational happiness. The prayer is for God to continue preparing His Good Girls and Good Guys and allowing them to cross each other's paths. As an unmarried man, I share in the same challenges as you to manage my physical desires while pursuing after God's righteousness. It's not easy and was never meant to be after the fall of man, but that is what will make each of us appreciate the treasure at the end of the journey.

Chapter 39

Is Love a Fantasy or Reward?

Is 21st century love a fantasy or a reward for dedication, perseverance and hard work?

Television shows, movies and romance novels paint the experiences of love through fantasies seemingly available to anyone who desires them. However, are these sources of inspiration only spreading false hope to those mesmerized by the mere thought of becoming the lead character in their favorite fantasy? There is an abundance of hopeless romantics who live life with the expectation of realities that will never come to pass.

Does love at first sight really exist? Or should people focus more on love through relationship development?

Many men and women begin down the road of relationships pursuing the preconceived desires of love. Upon further reflection, usually when desperation begins, many recognize what they sought never really existed in modern day society. I recently had an opportunity to speak with a close friend of mine who referred to his current relationship as 'highly tolerable.' Unfortunately, this wasn't the first time I'd heard such a description of a relationship. Many people, especially men, are now approaching relationships with a perspective of tolerance rather than an expectation of greater purpose and happiness.

Men are now opting to find women who serve as better life business partners, rather than those who fulfill the ever-elusive stereotype portrayed in movies, music videos and professional sports. Women are now opting for men who serve as emotional supporters, rather than the ever-elusive stereotype promoted via popular entertainment outlets. Some people may argue that love based on fantasies are fewer in number than those that develop through hard work and dedication. What are your thoughts on love as a fantasy or reward?

'Do It' Standing Up Point of Application

The fantasy of love is that it exists without hard work, ups and downs, or times of frustration and selflessness. If you believe you can have true love without the aforementioned characteristics, you're headed for disappointment. Love is a reward! It's a reward for those willing to put in hard work, which is dedicated and willing to exist in life situations outside of themselves. Are you willing to make yourself a factor in the reward of love? I pray that you are!

100

Chapter 40

Is Jesus All It Takes?

I am intrigued by the many bible thumpers, who are professing to be more spiritual than everyone else; who often say that ALL relationships will be successful if two people both 'have Jesus.' While I do agree with this thought in theory, implementing this perspective into practice is a much more arduous task. In a personal relationship with Christ you receive salvation and begin the daily journey of personal life transformation. This individual relationship allows you to go through the ups and down of life inclusive of the lessons God wants YOU to personally experience. However, it is much deeper when you try to bring two individual followers of Christ together in pursuit of covenant relationship. How simple and awesome would it be to have successful marriages solely created by bringing two believers together? By the 55%[+] divorce among evangelical Christians, we see that simply 'having Jesus' is not the only necessary element for experiencing successful relationships and marriages.

Please don't mistake what I'm saying; Christ is the most important foundational component of all relationships (Amos 3:3, 2 Corinthians 6:14-15). However, there are character, interpersonal and relational components that also play a part in building successful relationships and marriages involving two mutually exclusive individuals.

'Do It' Standing Up Point of Application

Do not be misled into thinking that if you find another believer, then marital bliss is right around the corner. If successfully coming together with a mate in a relationship were easy, then everyone would be doing it. Unfortunately, 'having Jesus' is only the beginning to a long journey of ongoing relationship maintenance and development. Following Jesus allows you to navigate through the ups and downs associated with relationship development. Don't get discouraged...pack your bags and prepare for the journey because it is going to be fun!

Chapter 41

For Better or For Worse

'Tis the season for marital issues in the lives of a few close friends. When the stresses of life intertwine with the intimate interaction of marriage, it is very easy to see how relationships can begin to experience strain. The covenant of marriage states that marriage is for better or for worse, but how many people actually look forward to persevering through the second part of that statement? Enjoying the 'better' part of relationships is the easy part. However, it's amazing how two people can get along harmoniously for weeks or months at a time, but short-term interruptions in this flow of harmony can cause two people to reconsider their commitment to one another. Unfortunately, many people become lured by the 'better' clause of the covenant statement, but fail to really understand the 'worse' clause of the covenant statement.

I now know why the courtship process is so important in assessing the potential reality of two people becoming one through marriage. Courtship allows two individuals to go through an ongoing set of real life interviews to determine if they are right for one another. Unfortunately, courtship in the eyes of some is seen as a race to the altar. However, in the attempt to race to the altar many lose sight of the little things that can cause problems later. A wise man once said that you shouldn't rush a person to the altar with the intent on altering them.

When assessing a potential mate for marriage, a person must realize a man or woman isn't like a pair of jeans, shoes or jacket that can be returned to a store in exchange for money back. You have to be willing to accept the person that stands across from you for who they are on your wedding day for better and for worse. If the person you marry is a cheater, then you must be open to the fact that he or she may continue cheating. If the person you marry is selfish, then you must be open to the reality that he or she may continue being selfish. If the person you marry is materialistic, then he or she may continue being materialistic. You marry both the good and the bad in a person. Also, understand that marriage will magnify the shortcomings in each person. You have to come to accept a person for who they are in their entirety.

'Do It' Standing Up Point of Application

Men and women are free-willed individuals who think, behave and operate according to where they are in life. God is the only one capable of changing a person's heart, desires and behavior. God accepts all of us in our humanity for better and for worse, so as believers we should follow in His footsteps and do the same.

Chapter 42

Change the Marriage Trend

When my parents celebrated their 39th wedding anniversary, I had the opportunity to speak with them. As I sat and listened to them speak about the longevity of their marriage, one thing that became clear was the fact that there is no way of escaping hard work in marriage. As I listened, I realized that no matter how much I speak about keys to relationships, preparing for relationships and understanding key indicators in relationships; nothing truly substitutes for experience and hard work.

As a youngster, I remember seeing my parents argue and engage in intense debates because of differing opinions. However, they were always able to reconcile and reach an understanding even if it meant agreeing to disagree. My parents' marriage was far from perfect, and through it all they both had spiritually grounded accountability partners that could help them navigate through times when they didn't want to be bothered with one another. As I listened and reflected, it became very apparent that throughout the duration of their marriage, divorce was never an option. Even if they thought about it, it was quickly dismissed and the process of reconciliation became the primary focus.

Having seen this parent model growing up, and seeing both sets of my grandparents remain married through the tests of time, I wondered if there may be a fear of marriage failure embedded deep within me. I needed to channel what could be fear into faith so I can live out my God-given purpose of redirecting views of marriage. We do live in a society that offers $300 divorces in case things don't work out. We live in a society where the generation of broken homes is now the norm for those within the 25 to 45 age group. The 'till death you part' generation is quickly fading off and we are in dire need of people to take and accept the challenge. We need to redirect our views of marriage and the impact healthy marriages have on our communities. Are you up for it? I am!

'Do It' Standing Up Point of Application

Begin viewing all of your future relationships through the lens of lifetime commitment. As your relationships become more serious, begin probing your significant other's thoughts on marriage and whether they see it as a lifelong commitment. Let's begin taking steps to change the disturbing trend that has now infected our society. Strong relationships lead to strong marriages. Strong marriages lead to strong families. Strong families lead to strong communities. Our households will benefit. Our communities will improve. Our lives will be blessed and God will be glorified!

Chapter 43

What's Love Got To Do With It?

It's interesting that a four-letter word has such an impact, both positive and negative, on the lives of people all across the world. Unfortunately, the thing that most people chase (love) is the one thing that many cannot define. Now, some of you may respond to me by saying there is no true way to define love and I will somewhat agree with you. However, if so many of us desire this pure essence called love for relationships, then we must be able to put our arms around what it looks like so we will recognize it when it manifests itself in our lives. I have asked many singles groups to define what love is and many sit there in amazement because they have never put much thought into the question.

More songs have been written about love than any other topic. Love has been the bond between husbands and wives, parents and children, brothers and sisters and lovers since the beginning of time. Love has also been the source of many broken hearts, relationships and families. However, love in its purest form doesn't disappoint people; people who misuse and abuse the concept of love disappoint people.

How can people unite together in holy matrimony all over the country without being able to truly define what love is? Could this be why the divorce rate in our country is above 50% and the family structure has collapsed right before our eyes?

Love in the original form has been associated with physical desires (eros), esteem and affection (philos), but is more appropriately described as unconditional (agape).

Let's take a brief look at what true love IS NOT!

1) **True love IS NOT solely based on feelings** – We all know that feelings are subject to change, so love based on emotional feelings is like a rollercoaster ride filled with ups and downs, but eventually comes to an end. This puts us in the mindset that love can be turned on and off with the press of a button. This is an inadequate depiction of the love you and I should be trying to experience. Yes, the degree to which you love someone may vary, but the core fire that ignites love within you cannot be extinguished.

2) **True love IS NOT about what you receive** – I've heard examples in the gossip circles (barber and beauty salons) about how someone displays love through the purchase of gifts and other material items. Any clown can purchase gifts, but you have to ask was the gift purchased to evoke a response? If the gift was purchased in exchange for future sex or favors, then the recipient is nothing more than a glorified prostitute. The definition of prostitute means someone who gives sex in exchange for compensation.

3) **True love IS NOT solely physical** – I have counseled countless women who have said they associate love with sex. This is an unfortunate occurrence that usually happens because love has not been properly modeled in the family environment in which they grew up. Men are also violators of this behavior. As mentioned in the previous point, love is not solely identified with sex. Sex is an expression of love between two people who are in a covenant relationship with one another. Notice I said covenant, but that's a different conversation.

4) **True love IS NOT conditional** – I once told an ex-girlfriend that I would love her if she stopped wasting her life away pursuing hopeless endeavors and decided to pursue a corporate career. At the time I made this statement, I believed that love could be conditioned based on the involvement of two parties. However, as we will see below, love is extended to others without regard to their response to us. If anyone states that they will love you 'IF' or 'But', then stop them in the midst of their statement and tell them to 'kick rocks' and keep it moving.

Let's take a brief dive into defining what true love does look like! The best description of love is found in the book of 1 Corinthians 13: 4-7. Unfortunately, my analysis of the characteristics of true love will have to be accomplished in a summary. Please allow this set of love characteristics to jumpstart your mind on being able to identify true expressions of love.

1) **True love is patient** – Even when you feel like forcefully expressing yourself. Love bears pain or trials without complaint, shows forbearance under provocation or strain, and is steadfast despite opposition, difficulty, or adversity.

2) **True love is kind** – Even when you want to retaliate physically or tear down another with your words. Love is sympathetic, considerate, gentle and agreeable.

3) **True love is not jealous** – Especially when you are aware that others are being noticed more than you. Love does not participate in rivalry, is not hostile toward one believed to enjoy an advantage, and is not suspicious. Love works for the welfare and good of others.

4) **True love does not brag** – Love does not flaunt itself boastfully and does not engage in self-glorification. Instead, love lifts and builds up others.

5) **True love is not arrogant** – Even when you think you are right and others are wrong. Love does not assert itself or become overbearing in dealing with others.

6) **True love does not act unbecomingly** – Even when being boastful, rude or overbearing will get you attention and allow you to get your own way. Love conforms to what is right, fitting and appropriate to the situation in order to honor the Lord.

7) **True love does not seek its own** – Biblical love is not selfish and self-seeking. True love does not try to fulfill its own desires, does not ask for its own way, and does not try to acquire gain for itself. Love is an act of the will, which seeks to serve and not be served.

8) **True love is not provoked** – Even when others attempt to provoke you or you are tempted to strike out at something or someone. Love is not aroused or incited to outbursts of anger. Love continues faithfully and gently to train others in righteousness, even when they fail.

'Do It' Standing Up Point of Application

I pray these characteristics of love help you begin to shape your ability to define what true love looks like and how to embrace love upon its arrival in your life. It's imperative that you begin to form your own understanding of what love is based on instructions from God who truly demonstrates what love looks like in our lives everyday.

Chapter 44

Do You Have A Solid Relationship Plan?

Why do so many people try to pursue relationships and marriages when they have never seen a successful one modeled before their eyes?

I just had a revelation about why the failure rate of relationships and marriages is at an all-time high. Unfortunately, we have an ever-increasing population of people who have never seen successful relationships and marriages lived out before them. It's sort of like trying to build a home with no blueprint. When you try build a house with no blueprint you are destined to fail. The complexity of such constructions makes it very difficult to build a quality product without specific directions. Similarly, relationships are complex entities that are difficult to build without a stable plan or set of instructions. What happens when two people disagree on a particular point? They each argue from their individual experience or historical point of view, which is dangerous. Unfortunately, two individuals arguing relationship perspectives from an experiential point of view often assist in destroying the long-term success of the relationship.

How can you argue about what makes a relationship successful, or validate your points of contention, when your points of reference are past failed relationships?

If you don't have any successful relationships from your past to reflect upon during your pursuit of relationship/marriage, I can offer a couple of suggestions:

1) **Read the Bible.** The Bible gives foundational components of successful

relationships. The core characteristics of healthy relationships are agape love, giving, selflessness, reconciliation and communication. John 3:16 is great biblical evidence on how relationships should be modeled.

2) **Seek relationship/marriage mentors.** A great source for understanding relationships issues are couples whose relationships have withstood the test of time. Things will go wrong in your relationships, but not all conflicts are worth risking the loss of your relationship/marriage. You have to learn which issues lack importance and which ones are detrimental to a relationship.

3) **Work on you.** It is very difficult to operate in a relationship when you have not purged your baggage from previous relationships. Contrary to your biological clock, the latest magazine story or what the media says, you are better off by yourself, than connected to someone who makes your joined relationship unhealthy.

'Do It' Standing Up Point of Application

Healthy relationships require two people dedicated to a life of ongoing love, selflessness and communication. In order to assist with the process of developing strong relationships, you need a strong relationship plan, good mentors and a spiritual conviction that declares divorce is not an option!

Chapter 45

Managing Expectations

One of my most popular sayings is "Disappointment comes when your reality doesn't measure up to your expectations." Unfortunately, you can't totally control your reality, but you can better manage your expectations. Don't get me wrong; it's only human for us to generate some level of expectation for certain things in our lives. However, we do own responsibility for the amount of faith we place in our expectations in comparison to how we prepare for the reality of what happens when the results are received.

There are typically two results that occur when dealing with your expectations:

1) **Happiness** - Happiness occurs when a reality in your life (e.g. event, relationship, activity) meets or exceeds your expectations.

2) **Disappointment** - Disappointment occurs when a reality in your life (e.g. event, relationship, activity) does not meet, or falls below your expectations.

'Do It' Standing Up Point of Application

The best way of dealing with both happiness and disappointment is to identify a method to properly manage your expectations. The best way to manage your expectations is to recognize that you do not have the ability to change or control people or situations. Once you recognize that God is in control of everything that happens in your life, you will be better equipped to deal with both happiness and disappointment.

Here are two verses that keep me grounded when either happiness or disappointment surfaces in my life:

Psalm 118:24 - This is the day the LORD has made; let us rejoice and be glad in it.

Psalm 30:5 - Weeping may endure for a night, But joy comes in the morning.

Chapter 46

Perspective of LOVE

There are some very distinct differences between how men and women view and grow into LOVE.

It has been stated that women fall in LOVE and men sort of grow into LOVE over time. Men really have to choose to LOVE someone because we are taught in our youthful years to flee from or suppress our emotions. In spite of our ability to camouflage our emotions, we basically know within the first couple of months of dating/courting whether we are interested in pursuing a long-term relationship. Men find someone who they consider attractive and then seek to grow into LOVE over time. Women on the other hand, typically find a man who they view as quality and seek to confirm their LOVE interest in them. Women can become progressively attracted to a man over a short period of time.

I used to wonder why I would often see attractive women with men who society would view as 'average'. It is because the 'average' man displayed quality characteristics that led the woman to become progressively attracted to them.

- **Women** – Do you agree that men of quality become more attractive over time?
- **Men** – Do you know if you're in it for the long haul early on in the relationship? Does anything really change for you after a couple months of dating a woman?

'Do It' Standing Up Point of Application

This chapter is solely intended to generate healthy discussion between you and your friends. It's always a great way to initiate a conversational exchange between men and women at your next house gathering or social event. Men

115

and women have very different perspectives of love and it's always fun to take part in passionate discussions that help bridge understandings between the opposite sexes.

Chapter 47

Real Men Take Risks!

One thing I am learning as I travel this journey called life is being a Christian doesn't offer me an excuse for not being a man. As I study and read God's Word, and even watch what's going on in our society, we desperately need men who are willing to get back to the basics of what manhood is. One element of being a man involves taking risks.

As God's mighty creation, He expects us to take charge and fulfill our roles as head of the household. Unfortunately, there are many of us who are willing to take risks professionally, financially and socially, but aren't willing to do so relationally. One of the detriments of having the number of women to men odds in our favor is our tendency to lay back and wait until women throw themselves at our feet for attention. Like many of my brothers, I embraced this royal treatment and soon recognized that I didn't have to do much except sit back and benefit. I realized during that phase (notice I said 'phase') of my life I picked up some habits that were detrimental to God-centered relationship development.

As long as I continued to live according to my own selfish agenda, I found myself never having to take risks or make challenging relationship decisions. Why settle down? Why commit? Why explain myself to those I was dating? Those were questions I often pondered, but never felt a responsibility to address. I left many decisions suspended in mid-air because I found myself wanting to remain comfortable and keep those around me happy. As long as I remained focused on pleasing people instead of God, I found myself out of alignment with His purpose for my life.

'Do It' Standing Up Point of Application

Being a real man means making tough choices and taking selfless risks. Once you realize the call God has on your life, being His chosen leader for the family household requires you to take risks and make difficult decisions. It's only when you realize the responsibility God has bestowed upon you that you can stop playing games with the women in your life and focus on building the best possible relationship with the ONE woman He blesses you with.

The woman you marry will look to you to lead, sacrifice, offer a selfless perspective and offer a big picture view according to what's best for the entire family. The role of being a man, leader and head of the household, involves an ongoing process of taking risks and making difficult decisions. A real man is willing to approach a woman and risk rejection. A real man is willing to make tough professional decisions. A real man is willing to make decisions that may result in failure. A real man is willing to make decisions that may not be popular with friends or family. Are you willing to take risks that will allow God to mature you into the man He desires for you to be?

Chapter 48

My Parting Thoughts

Now that you have arrived at this point in the book it means you have completed all of the chapters. I know you may still be asking yourself what is the point of "Can You Do It Standing Up? A Different Position On Relationships?" Well, hopefully reading Can You Do It Standing Up? has challenged you to take a look at self-development, communication, love and commitment along with others in a new or different way. We can no longer continue down the current path of marriages and relationships we see today.

I am tired of seeing relationships fail because two broken people try to come together as a solution to their issues. I am tired of seeing selfishness serve as the catalyst of destroying marriages. This ugly and progressive trend can end if each of us takes personal responsibility for addressing our self-development areas, while encouraging those in our circles of influence to do the same.

I know some of my thoughts and perspectives may seem radical and that is okay. Vision allows me to see something that others cannot. My vision is the following:

- More men and women desiring monogamous committed relationships
- More unmarried men and women serving in the church and in the community
- More men and women focused on giving to others rather than taking for themselves
- More open public communication about relationship issues
- No more failed marriages due to irreconcilable differences
- No more hurt women at the hands of insufficient knowledge

Are you interested in seeing the same? Well partner with me by seizing the opportunity to share this message with others. Together, WE can positively change the current course of relationships if we trust God, focus on developing ourselves and surround ourselves with positive people. Believe in God; believe in yourself, the best is still yet to come!

ABOUT THE AUTHOR

Kenny Pugh is the Founder of Kenny Pugh, L.L.C., the platform on which Kenny exercises a versatile professional life as a consultant, coach, and speaker. Kenny Pugh, L.L.C. is the sponsoring company for Chat Kafe, where Kenny offers relationship advice, writes inspirational blogs, and hosts his weekly internet radio program, The Chat Kafe Show with Kenny Pugh (www.chatkafeonline.com).

Through years of experience as a facilitator, workshop presenter, and keynote speaker at various conferences, ministry services, and for-profit corporate events, Kenny has refined his sense of the art of communication and the power of relationships. With the knowledge and vision to explore the common hardships of life and unfold them through communication, Kenny found his life's purpose by helping others restore the foundations of their many relationships. Now, his mission is to encourage, empower, and equip people to reach their God-given potential through public speaking and personal coaching.

Kenny believes in presenting information in a manner that is simple, practical, and easy to understand, and his teachings have touched on a variety of key topics, such as effective leadership, interpersonal relationships, sexual purity, and home buying and credit management. He has published several articles related to his spiritual knowledge of relationships and financial knowledge of the credit industry.

Kenny wishes to serve as a vessel of understanding in an era of disconnected, aimless, and broken relationships, and to soothe adversities of all forms, whether practical, relational, or spiritual. To accomplish this goal, he offers a full line of services, including speaking, coaching, consulting, online media, literature, events, and more. To partner with Kenny Pugh, please visit his website at www.kennypugh.com for more information.

15801230R40065

Made in the USA
Charleston, SC
21 November 2012